C000230815

LED BY THE LAND

LANDSCAPES BY KIM WILKIE

Kim Wilkie

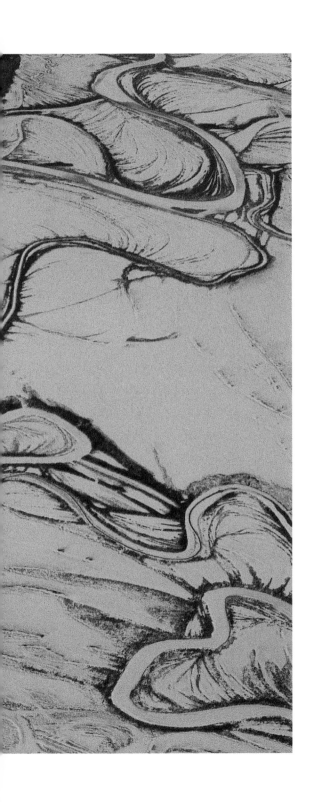

LED BY
THE LAND

LANDSCAPES BY
KIM WILKIE

PIMPERNEL
PRESS LTD
www.pimpernelpress.com

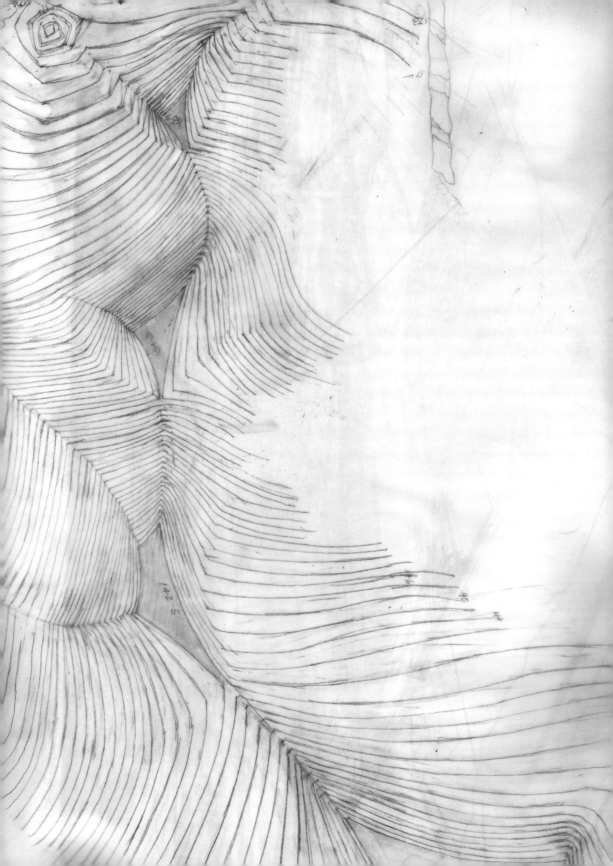

CONTENTS

FOREWORD

BY DIETER HELM

The landscape we know is man-made. It is organic: it has, at least until the last couple of centuries, evolved as a gradual symbiosis between us humans and its natural capital, of which we are a part. It is not wild and it has not been 'wild' for millennia. Wild, in the sense of non-human, passed away long ago. Returning to the 'wild', leaving humans out, is to suggest a value for nature's sake and not our own. Nature doesn't care: we do, or at least we should.

Landscapes have been sculpted by this symbiosis. We have, in Kim Wilkie's terms, been 'led by the land', and the particular form of the moulding of the land by us is as important as the design of the built environment. There is no blank canvas: it is already populated. The buildings we create sit in the land. We add to what is already there. When we respect the natural processes and what our predecessors have done, the results can be stunning – as the photographs in this book show. The contrast between what Kim Wilkie has achieved, and so much of the brutalisation of the land through intensive farming and many housing estates plonked down without regard to their surroundings, is stark – whether it be in the approach to his own farm or the design for the Fawley Waterside project he is currently working on.

The unifying theme which runs through Kim Wilkie's work is a positive and progressive one. It is one of optimism, not despair. His hero is Alexander Pope, whose enlightenment philosophy placed humans back at the participating centre of nature. It is this enlightenment spirit rather than the often anti-humanism of some romantics and many environmentalists that sets his work apart. Wordsworth wanted to keep the railway out of his beloved Lake District, for fear of the people who might also enjoy the natural capital he so valued. Kim Wilkie does not want to keep people out. Whether it is the Transylvanian village, the urban space outside County Hall in London, the vertical green walls of the Longwood Gardens in Pennsylvania, or the stunning formalism of the landscaping at Boughton House, all his projects are ultimately full of optimism about what we can be and what we can become. There is spirit here. Led by the land yes, but not constrained by its current state.

Building on the past does not mean nostalgia. We are the product of our past. We have history, and that history shapes our understanding and it is the platform upon which to build our future. That is the great insight of historians. Even revolutions get brought down to earth, our earth. It is not hard to deduce that Kim Wilkie is an historian by training. The natural capital that we have inherited has been fundamental to the great economic transformation since 1800, and especially since 1900. The enlightenment brought us back into nature, but it has also given us a science with which to both build and destroy. There is little doubt that we have done a lot of destruction, but it does not have to be this way.

The sense of place and harmony that Kim Wilkie's examples gives us is in stark contrast to the destruction all around us. The great challenge of our time is how to stop wrecking biodiversity and the climate, to respect natural capital and not to destroy it. It is to redirect the principles of the enlightenment to make us more enlightened about which path to follow. If we are not led by the land, we will be led further towards the destruction of more and more nature. This is not going to end well.

Taking the right enlightenment path is about much more than protecting iconic species and investing in renewable energy technologies. It requires thinking about systems, not marginal projects. It has to be an integrated approach, and it will have to build on what we have inherited. The core natural capital processes underpin the production of food from our soils and water, trees and plants clean up our air, and they can yield the sustainably and complex ecosystems, without which life will become 'nasty, brutish and short'.

Imagine what we could have instead of what we have brought about. Look at the wonderful photographs and illustrations in this book, and contrast these with some of the barrenness of many urban landscapes and the green and golden deserts and rows of plantation trees we have forced on the countryside. We can have a green and pleasant land; it can be green and prosperous too. It is in our interests to follow Pope and put ourselves back in the multiple landscapes that we can create and improve. It is a process of science and art, which is the heart of a proper enlightenment.

There are multiple dimensions to making this happen. It is about economics and the proper inclusion of all the aspects of our lives in economic calculations. It is not the poverty of the imagination that GDP measures, but rather a comprehensive account of human welfare and flourishing. We are part of nature, and we need nature to fully realise our potential. It is not an accident that 'green' is crucial to our mental health, soothing our stressed lives. Science has demonstrated this, and the art of landscapes is part of its delivery.

What Kim Wilkie gives us is part of the template – insights into how to reshape our relationship with nature, give it back its form and shape, and in the process bring us both use and delight. It is nature with a purpose, not a romantic return to some primitive state of nature. It is the antithesis to treating our waterways as sewers, our seas as rubbish dumps and our land as the blotting paper for chemicals. It is creating a sense of useful and beautiful harmony. We debate a great deal about the architecture of the built environment, and look at endless designs of buildings. But we can't understand these as separate from the landscape. All of Kim Wilkie's examples here are about this relationship.

HALF-TITLE PAGE The Orphean pool at Boughton House.
TITLE PAGE Meandering and braided rivers of ice in Canada.
PAGE 4 Sketch for landforms at Fulford.

INTRODUCTION

We used to live in a house on stilts by the edge of the jungle. There was no glass in the windows, just heavy, slatted shutters that we scrambled to close when a tropical storm broke. Lavatory paper had to be locked away because the monkeys loved to swing through the house, scoop up the rolls and festoon them through the treetops. There were umbrellas of bamboo and waxed paper furled in the corridors to protect us from the fruit bats that flew through the rooms dropping bombs of bright effluent.

It was a childhood of intense images – butterflies, orchids, cowries and temples – dense with colour and smell. Things decayed as fast as they grew. Climbing plants felt as though they could scale a house overnight, covering the meagre man-made things inside that rotted as rapidly as the vines advanced. Leather shoes would fur over with blue mould in hours and SAS ants would carry off any food left unguarded. This was nature at its most mischievous. It had pace.

From Malaysia we moved to Iraq. The desert was complete peace; it felt slow and pale and eternal. The sky was huge, with comets passing coolly through the night. Nothing rotted and it never seemed to rain. Most of the winter my friends and I were out in the desert looking for traces of former lives. Ancient Mesopotamian cities can be picked out as abandoned mounds and we spent days walking slowly over the surface searching for fragments from millennia ago. The wind would blow the sand and reveal a Roman coin, a Phoenician glass bead or the corner of a tablet with cuneiform script. Everything was bleached brown. Staring at a patch of ground for hours would reveal nothing and then all of a sudden the shape of an ear on a little figurine or the iridescence of a shard of glass from a tear vase would come into focus. The waste ground turned into treasure and you could touch a handle that someone had grasped five thousand years ago, just lying forgotten on the surface of the desert.

Those extremes of land, water and human occupation gave me a vivid sense of landscape. From typhoons to sand storms, violent weather held a thrill. We also lived in Hong Kong for a time, and I remember staring from our little bungalow in Sek Kong for two days as Typhoon Wanda ripped off our neighbours' roofs and hurled boats inland. I was watching from the protection of childhood, where flying roofs looked like magic and monsoon

Franklin Farm, Hampshire.

drains became water flumes that my sister and I could ride down the valley. Violent weather now holds a deeper threat and its awe is more savage.

Coming to England was in its way as disconcerting as the move from jungle to desert. We arrived in the Big Freeze of 1962, one of the coldest winters on record in the United Kingdom. My parents rented a house without central heating and then, after a year, left me in a boarding school that was equally casual about the cold. But I became captivated by bonfires, farm life and the gentleness of sounds in mist and twilight.

My picture of the world formed within that triangle of climates and cultures, always surrounded by animals. In Malaysia I wallowed in mud with parrots; in Iraq I carved miniature cities out of cliffs of compacted sand with a mongoose; and in England I learned to grow plants and tend cows. But perhaps most significant of all was the long-term reaction to a nomadic early life. When we finally settled on a small farm in Hampshire, I put down a tap root that tethers deep.

I didn't discover landscape architecture until I was twenty-one and in my last year of a degree in modern history at Oxford. It came as a revelation. I could hardly believe that everything I loved could be wrapped up in one profession: land, stories, biology and drawing. I have been led on from there.

My understanding of landscape architecture is close to the vision of Slartibartfast, who designed small planets in Douglas Adams's *Hitchhiker's Guide to the Galaxy*. It touches on everything from farming, forestry and mining to how we plan our streets and cemeteries. Deep down it depends on collaboration – and some negotiation – with the natural and cultural forces that shape the environment. In this book I hope to give a sense of the enormous scope and excitement that the work involves. This second edition is updated with fresh projects, themes from my articles in the *Financial Times* and the optimism of growing older.

For something so rooted in a fixed place, our perception of landscape is surprisingly fluid. It is a kind of riddle, changing with every cloud and mood, and yet appearing timeless and stationary. There is a continuous conversation between the great geologic crust of the Earth and the tiny details on its surface – the bustling lives lived and shaped upon it. To understand landscape, you need to grasp the immensity of time and follow the natural flows of land, water and people. These flows leave a sediment of memories accumulating in each place. Working with landscape is as much about ideas and attitudes as physical form. And it is probably more about how the land is used and organized, than what it looks like. At base, landscape is profoundly political: how we share natural resources between all living things.

In Britain, the attitude to landscape has been greatly influenced by the eighteenth-century English Enlightenment and the writing of Alexander Pope. England went off in a different direction from the Continent and North America, where Jean-Jacques Rousseau and the Romantic idea of untrammelled Wilderness were more powerful. Pope was part of a philosophical and scientific shift that placed humans back at a participating centre of nature, rather than allowing them an elegant separation from the natural world behind baroque patterns and divine benediction. It was the moment, at a new distance from the Abrahamic faiths, when magic met science. The combination of Isaac Newton and Alexander Pope was potent. Pope revived the classical nature gods of the Renaissance as a mystical metaphor and revealed beauty in well-farmed land. When Newton died in 1727, Pope wrote this epitaph:

NATURE and Nature's Laws lay hid in Night:
God said, 'Let Newton be!' and all was light.

The garden historian Mavis Batey introduced me to the subtleties of Pope and the clarity of his ideas about the natural world. As a young woman, Mavis was one of the key Enigma Code-crackers for Churchill at Bletchley Park. She had a mind that remembered everything and wove disparate strands together in patterns of great insight. Mavis explained Pope's understanding of landscape as poetry modulated by the day-to-day practicalities of surviving on the land. In his fourth epistle to Burlington in 1731 he wrote: '*All must be adapted to the Genius and the Use of the Place, and the Beauties not forced into it, but resulting from it.*' The '*Genius of the Place*' has become something of a catch phrase to cover the intrinsic character and personality of a site; but the '*Use*' bit is usually forgotten. Pope was stressing that the way we live on the land – the need to interact with food, water and shelter – is as critical to design as how we feel about it. The basic operations of human existence were to be acknowledged and enjoyed as part of life and landscape.

This early eighteenth-century English Landscape Movement conjured up the classical Arcadian concept of mankind working in peaceful harmony with pastoral nature. It was based on the animated prospect of people living side by side with animals. The view out from the garden into the productive countryside became as important as the elegant garden itself. The subsequent Picturesque Movement, responding to a more suburban patronage, concentrated on the painterly qualities of landscape and focused on wild scenes of rocks and blasted trees rather than pastoral bliss. It left humans once again separate from, rather than part of, the landscape: observers removed from its earthy inner workings.

The Arcadian appreciation of landscape has come and gone over the centuries, but it feels particularly relevant now that we appear to be at a turning point. Abrupt and radical shifts in climate, finance and politics have unsettled our view of the world and its future. Together, they make an alarming mix. While living standards have generally appeared to get better and better, there has been little incentive to change our habits. Although concern about climate change has been temporarily overwhelmed by worries about money and politics, our assumptions about growth and the way that we survive on the planet are all now freshly challenged. The debate needs to develop beyond carbon to the way that we actually live. We have a chance to question some of the twentieth-century fundamentals of economics. Is it possible, for example, to pursue growth in fulfilment rather than growth in accumulation? Can we channel our energy into improving the quality of our lives rather than increasing the quantity of our possessions?

In the twists and turns of justice and politics, landscape architecture has a few insistent issues to raise. Some sort of sensible stewardship of the land has to be at the basis of any political and financial solution. How should we grow our food? How can we store water and energy locally and distribute them more fairly? What sort of buildings should be built and where? How can we cohabit with one another and nature? How do we stay sane? Can we hold on to the wit and spirit of what has gone before and let it inspire new ideas and design?

These questions are the basics of landscape architecture and this book tries to look at some of the issues raised in my work over the last three decades. It starts with land and water. The sacred Russian monastery of Solovki presents life on the edge of existence. For five thousand years, human civilization has managed to cling to the rim of the Arctic Circle, gathering food, light and inspiration in a climate where humans struggle to survive each winter. It is a place of brutality and belief. The Saxon villages of Transylvania work on the same careful principles of stewardship, but are more challenged by politics and economics than climate. These are places of magical and monstrous histories that show how mere survival can frame landscape, buildings and beliefs.

Back in England, the Thames Landscape Strategy makes a striking contrast, exploring the evolution of a rich, fertile river valley and its ability to infuse a culture and an empire. It links to a repeating Arcadian idyll that, in varying shades, has obsessed the Augustan poets of Rome, the Florentine Renaissance, the English Enlightenment and contemporary ideas on sustainability in Europe and America. My projects at Villa La Pietra in Florence, the Oxford and Moscow botanic gardens and Longwood Gardens in Pennsylvania explore these ideas of water, soil and food.

From land and water, we move to life: wild and human. Wet meadows around Winchester demonstrate an ancient relationship between wildlife and agriculture. The chalk streams of Hampshire provide some of the rarer habitats in the world and I look at how landownership, management and design can combine to create a precious landscape of arrested adolescence. In other words, how to manage rich young habitats like wet meadows in order to keep them open rather than letting them gradually transform into dense woodland. The transformation of the grounds around the Natural History Museum in London has given the opportunity to look at life on Earth from deep time to an urbanized future. While across the road, the stories of human culture have shaped the spaces at the Victoria and Albert Museum and the war memorials of Hyde Park Corner. Finally, the community garden of Hyde Abbey in Winchester, Maggie's Centre in Swansea and ideas for burying the dead in the City of London Cemetery consider urban spaces in differing complexities.

More recently, my work has concentrated on new settlements. The pressures to find space for housing, water and food may at first seem to be in competition, but the redevelopment of Chelsea Barracks in London and the new towns of Madinat al Irfan in Oman and Fawley Waterside in Hampshire show some ways of combining these elements symbiotically.

The third part of the book concentrates on the spirit of design and the way it can link back to long traditions and retelling of stories. I explore a personal obsession with landform and the many ways that you can carve and mould the earth. Inspirations come from the deep British tradition of earthworks – Iron Age forts and burial mounds; the eighteenth-century land sculptures of Charles Bridgeman and John Aislabie; and the magical works of Andy Goldsworthy. They all seem connected in a beautifully tactile way and have helped to fuel my ideas for large landform projects across the world. Smaller and more playful projects include County Hall in London, the Vitsœ furniture factory in Leamington Spa and even my old studio in Richmond.

Lastly, I look at my own home ground and how the place has shaped the way I live and design. The relationship between farming, natural systems and wildlife is now my daily routine.

Franklin Farm, Hampshire.

LAND
AND WATER

In the total volume of the planet, we inhabit the thinnest layer on the surface of the sphere and rely on a meagre band of atmosphere that hovers above that layer. The cross-section through the Earth is 12,756 kilometres (7,926 miles), but the habitable crust is only 50 kilometres (31 miles) deep and the atmosphere is less than 12 kilometres (7.5 miles) high. This places life in a very fragile band around the planet. Landscape architecture has to start here, in this extraordinary film of biosphere.

Dried riverbed, Utah.

ON THE EDGE

Extremes of human existence throw the relationship with the biosphere into sharpest relief. Life on the edge of severe climate leaves little room for manoeuvre. Just securing food and shelter gives an acute awareness of the importance of land and water. It is revealing to see how settlements survive under these conditions and it highlights where our priorities might lie as climate change accelerates. Over the years, I have worked on a few projects that have shown great ingenuity in basic survival and long-term stewardship of the land. Two in particular – the Solovetsky Archipelago and the Saxon villages of Transylvania – give insights into the way that we might look at the principles of settlement afresh.

BELOW The Solovetsky Archipelago sits in the White Sea on the edge of the Arctic Circle. Great Muksalma Island is linked by a causeway to the main Bolshoi Solovetsky Island.

SOLOVKI

RUSSIA

The Solovki Transfiguration Cathedral built 1556–66 and recently restored after the destruction of the Gulag occupation. The monastery is one of the most sacred in Russia and was founded in 1436 by Saints Savvatii and Zosima.

The Solovetsky Archipelago has formed at the junction of tectonic plates in the White Sea on the edge of the Russian Arctic Circle. The Earth's crust is unusually thin at this point and geothermal heat reaches the surface, contributing to a microclimate that has helped humans to inhabit the remote islands for at least five thousand years. It is a place of spiritual intensity. Over the millennia, people have expressed their veneration in structures from early pagan stone labyrinths to one of the most sacred of the Russian monasteries. Solovki was also the first labour camp in the Soviet Gulag and a place of murder and torture.

LEFT, TOP The small wooden church of St Andrew, built by Peter the Great in 1702 on Great Zayatsky Island.

LEFT, BOTTOM The seventeenth-century causeway to Muksalma. The sinuous design acts as a breakwater, creating protected pockets for farming fish.

RIGHT The ice house used for preserving food in summer in the vegetable garden beside the Archimandrite's hermitage.

The journey to the archipelago is a little bit easier in summer when the sea has thawed from a wreckage of ice cliffs and crevasses to milky water, allowing boats to cross from the port of Kem on the Russian mainland. Even then it is not a simple journey. The train from Moscow to Kem takes twenty-five hours and the port is a grim, abandoned place of rusting metal. The boat that sets out towards the Arctic Circle seems to be heading off the edge of the world. Then, just as you think you'll never see land again, a tiny globe floats on the horizon. Slowly the globe rises out of the water on a white tower. More globes and towers gradually appear and finally the monastery becomes visible, balancing on a spit between the harbour and the Holy Lake. It seems to emerge straight from the water.

Solovki embodies life on the edge. In the fragile environment of the Far North, the monks evolved a system of land management from the fifteenth century onwards that was balanced at the limit of survival. They experimented with growing and storing sufficient food and fuel in summer to last them through the six months of dark isolation during the Arctic winter. They managed to drain enough bogs, to grow enough hay, to support enough cattle, to produce enough manure, to fertilize enough vegetables to survive. They knew just how much seaweed they could harvest without upsetting the micro-environment around the shore and they banned any logging of trees, only allowing collection of fallen dry wood for fuel. A small botanical garden was grown for medicines and for bees, as much to provide wax for candles and winter light as for honey.

The monastery was not just a group of islands of primitive subsistence: it became a religious and cultural focus of great significance. It was also a place of technology and innovation, constantly refining land management with engineering sophistication, while at the same time retaining a careful balance with natural systems. The network of fifty lakes, into which the bogs were drained, was in turn linked by canals to provide a flow of pure drinking water and ultimately hydro-electric power to the monastery. Even the causeways connecting the islands were designed as hydro-dynamic forms to moderate ocean currents for fish farming.

Solovki was much destroyed by the Soviet period and the brutal passage through the Gulag, but the monks have now returned and the archipelago has been recognized as a World Heritage Site. I was commissioned by The Prince of Wales's Business Leaders' Forum to provide initial advice on how to restore and sustain the historic cultural landscape. In many ways this project embodies the relationship between man, land and fragile cultural existence. I worked with the Russian botanist, Artyom Parshin, and my role as landscape architect was initially a kind of triage: to identify what was most significant, most vulnerable and most urgent to restore and repair. It was a delicate balancing of political, cultural and natural priorities. There were sensitive questions, such as which twentieth-century buildings should be removed to reveal the monastery in its dramatic setting, without distorting some of the darker history of the place, and how new facilities could be included

ABOVE Many of the 1950s buildings beyond the monastery are now empty and redundant. Their removal would help to repair the wild setting of the sixteenth-century cathedral complex and restore its relationship with the White Sea.

ABOVE One of the
Neolithic labyrinths that
still survive on Great
Zayatsky Island. Solovki
has been a sacred site for
thousands of years.

without destroying the harmony of the whole. Furthermore, the future of
the World Heritage Site, and indeed the monastery community, depend on a
viable economic solution. There are difficult decisions about the numbers and
types of visitors, residents and pilgrims allowed to travel to the archipelago,
weighing revenue and public access against impact on the natural and cultural
environment. As a start, in such a complex web of jurisdictions, expectations
and funding sources, I tried to capture the essences of the place in a brief
analysis that could stir the imagination and focus priorities.

TRANSYLVANIA

ROMANIA

The work in Solovki led to a similar project for another World Heritage Site, the Siebenburgen in Transylvania, for the Mihai Eminescu Trust and The Prince of Wales's Charitable Foundation. The Siebenburgen are a group of Saxon villages in the centre of Romania. A story goes that, when the Pied Piper led the children out of rat-infested Hamelin, he brought them to a new life in Transylvania. More prosaically, Lower Rhinelanders were invited by the Hungarian King Geza II in the twelfth century to colonize the south-eastern frontier of his country as a buffer zone against the invading Ottomans. These 'Saxons' were granted land and virtual autonomy by King Geza and they quickly established two hundred villages in the area.

The Saxon villages, community and way of life have changed remarkably little since the twelfth century, despite a violent and turbulent history. From 1241 onwards, the settlers faced raids by Mongols, Ottomans, Hungarians and Romanians and the plague. After the Second World War, the majority of the adult Saxon population was sentenced to seven years' hard labour in the Soviet Union and only about half of the deported Saxons survived to return to a Communist Romania. Then in 1990, following Ceausescu's removal from power, the Saxons were invited to repatriate to Germany, seven centuries after their original departure. There was a mass emigration, leaving the future of the villages very uncertain.

Astonishingly, the Saxon villages still just manage to survive as the closest thing to a medieval landscape in Europe. There is the remnant of a beautiful balance between settlement, cultivation and nature. In the gentle, rolling countryside, the villages are tucked economically into the valley folds and defensible, fortified church complexes stand at strategic highpoints.

The Saxon villages of Transylvania survive in medieval harmony with the land. Agriculture, wild flowers, farm animals, wildlife and humans are all mutually dependent.

Symmetrical patterns of terraced street houses, cobbled courtyards and wooden barns extend in strips up the valley sides through vegetable gardens, orchards and meadows to thickly wooded ridges. Everywhere there are animals: horses, cows, pigs and poultry in the villages; wolves, bears, lynx and wild boar in the forests; and eagles, owls, storks and larks in the skies. The meadows are lush with wild flowers and streams run fresh from hillside springs. The rhythm of grazing, haymaking and harvesting sets the pace of life. Each dawn in the village of Viscri a young boy leads the cattle out to pasture and the courtyard doors of the houses open for their cows to follow him in single file down the street. In the evening he returns and each cow peels off nonchalantly to her respective address, as the villagers welcome them back with a shot of local vodka. It is the kind of harmony of human settlement in nature that we can only dream about in the twenty-first century.

The villages are tucked into the folds of the land, facing on to an animal-dominated main street. Narrow street frontages open back to long parcels that rise through courtyards, stables, vegetable gardens, orchards and vineyards to the pasture and woods beyond. The village community is concentrated on the street and each plot relates equally up to the valley sides. The villages are a model of sustainable rural settlement, but the life is hard and the population ageing and thinning.

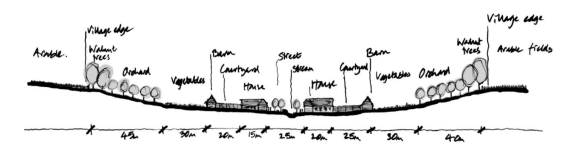

Since the 1990 exodus, the villages have emptied and the remaining communities are mostly elderly and impoverished. This, combined with Romania's entry into the European Union, the Common Agricultural Policy, the disbanding of the collective farms and the acquisition of large swathes of fertile land by foreign investors, means that the traditional labour-intensive methods of farming are becoming more tenuous. Most of all, the remnant population of the Saxon villages clearly wants to rise out of subsistence farming to enjoy the benefits of modern life.

My task was again to follow a triage of landscape assessment of the most significant, vulnerable and viable. I then had to help communicate a wider understanding of the unique value of the place. I was also asked to make suggestions for the full and healthy development of the communities that are an intrinsic part of the character and management of the landscape. The process was similar to Solovki, but the landscape is fundamentally different. In Transylvania, it is the typical rather than the unique that is significant. The consistent pattern of settlement in the landscape is even more special than individual flourishes. Most precious of all is the way of life, where centuries of careful management of the land and woods have led to a remarkable interaction of habitats. Human and wild life is interdependent. The wildflower meadows would revert to forest if they were not cut and harvested each year. The rich flora of the woods would be shaded out if the processes of thinning and coppicing were to stop. The complex ties of the community would be fundamentally changed if the shared and pervasive management of the land were to be transferred to a mechanized third party. Keeping some form of labour-intensive agriculture is the key to the survival of the remarkable landscape, as well as employment and community. The challenge is to stimulate sufficient local and specialist markets to keep farming viable, to use mechanization at a scale that does not destroy the land and to encourage the young to return to the villages.

There is no simple way to catapult the twelfth century into the twenty-first, keeping the best and leapfrogging the mistakes. Although it might feel as though Transylvania holds some magic recipe for the Arcadian ideal of living with the land, few of us would put up with the severity of that existence. The Mihai Eminescu Trust Whole Village Project tries to link every aspect of the community survival. It is largely run and organized by leading figures within the local community and addresses everything from healthcare and education to infrastructure and legal and political protection. My contribution was to attempt to highlight the most important and fragile aspects of the landscape and natural environment, while at the same time finding sensitive and economic ways of introducing running water, local natural sewage treatment, cooperative agriculture ventures, internet connections, outside funding possibilities and sympathetic architectural conservation. In almost every project the key is to help people see and choose what is special and then to explore ways in which those priorities might be achieved in the simplest, most straightforward and sensitive steps.

The agricultural methods have changed little since the Middle Ages and the wildflower hay meadows are some of the best in Europe. The challenge is to introduce mechanization in a way that makes life easier without destroying the soil structure and floral diversity that creates a landscape which is beautiful, productive and full of life.

WATER

Slowly but surely water has created most of the landscapes we inhabit. It erodes mountains, carves valleys and meanders at will across plains. While sculpting the form of the land from the raw material of geology, water also makes settlement possible in the landscapes that it creates. Fresh water for drinking and irrigation, combined with coastal and river transport, has determined the location of most towns and cities. London is a perfect example.

LEFT The *Thames Landscape Strategy, Hampton to Kew* frames policies that respond to the way that people experience and understand the city around the river. The words and the plans try to be as approachable as possible.

THAMES LANDSCAPE STRATEGY

LONDON

BELOW Syon House from Kew Gardens. The two estates were designed by Lancelot Brown to flow visually together and the grazed wet meadow beside the river is now a Site of Special Scientific Interest.

The River Thames lies at the physical and spiritual centre of London. The flow of water through the capital is a powerful natural force that links the city westwards to the centre of England and eastwards to the sea; it is London's original reason for being. The daily tidal rhythm changes the shape and size of the river hour by hour. As well as bringing light, space and wildlife into the centre of the city, the river offers a salutary reminder of flood and drought. London has less per capita annual rainfall than Israel, but if the Tidal Barrier were to fail the central corridor of the city could be flooded, threatening 1.25 million people, 400 schools, 16 hospitals, 13 mainline stations, 8 power stations and much of the Underground system.

The river changes character through London. From the estuary in the east, the marshes and industrial areas give way to docklands upstream of

the tidal barrier. Between Tower and Chelsea bridges, the centre of the city is denser but it turns greener and more residential towards Kew. Between Kew and Hampton, the Thames meanders through a unique landscape of parks, palaces and working communities, with Richmond at its centre.

The Thames Valley at Richmond was the cradle of the English Landscape Movement in the eighteenth century. With apparent mutual respect and affection, the wife and mistress of George II – Queen Caroline and Henrietta Howard – living on opposite banks of the river, joined forces to patronize a radical new landscape philosophy. They befriended and employed the leading landscape architects and thinkers of the time: Alexander Pope, Charles Bridgeman, William Kent and Lancelot 'Capability' Brown. Their projects along this stretch of the Thames set the pattern for a more natural and fluid appreciation of landscape. Views and vistas were carefully merged to create a pastoral landscape where garden, river, man and beast were part of a seamless whole. Alexander Pope was writing and experimenting on his own garden at Twickenham and, just after Pope's death, Horace Walpole began on Strawberry Hill, within sight of Pope's villa.

I became involved with this upper Arcadian stretch of the river more than a quarter of a century ago. It all started with a 'Thames Connections' exhibition by the Royal Fine Art Commission in 1991. The commissioners invited nine young architects and a landscape architect to come up with ideas for the river. Rather than look at a specific building project, I became fascinated by a bird's-eye view of the whole river and its interaction with the city. Looking at historic maps and paintings, it was possible to trace the way that the upstream section of the London Thames was linked by ancient sightlines and vistas that worked with the topography of the land and the bends in the river. The form of the land, the flow of the water and strategic sightlines have shaped the character and development of this part of London.

LEFT, TOP *Richmond Hill, on the Prince Regent's Birthday*, by Joseph Mallord William Turner, exhibited 1819.

LEFT, BOTTOM The view from Richmond Hill, protected by Act of Parliament in 1902 and restored as wildflower meadow in 2005.

An extraordinary sequence of views still survives that stretches right across London, linking Windsor Castle to a Neolithic barrow on the top of Richmond Hill to St Paul's Cathedral to Greenwich. More locally, a network of sightlines along avenues and mounts connected all the palaces and major houses in the first 18 kilometres (11 miles) of the city from Hampton Court to Kew Gardens. The rhythm of open space and working waterfronts that was established around these natural features, views and landownerships still sets the pattern of urban design today.

The exhibition provoked some interest in south-west London and members of the local community approached me to take the ideas further. Over a period of three years, with the help of a group of inspired and dedicated people, we managed to prepare the *Thames Landscape Strategy, Hampton to Kew*. It was a rather different way of looking at planning a city. Instead of analysing the place in terms of specialist layers of zoning, we explored the river landscape as a whole: what it looks and feels like and how it makes sense to the people who live and work there. The strategy was based on years of daily observation; interviews with over a hundred and eighty local interest groups and fifty official bodies; and extensive public consultation. It charted the historic, natural and recreation landscapes, crossing borough boundaries and legal jurisdictions to agree policies and projects for the next hundred years – the time it

BELOW Syon, Kew Gardens and the Richmond Old Deer Park are all connected by vistas and meridian lines along and across the river.

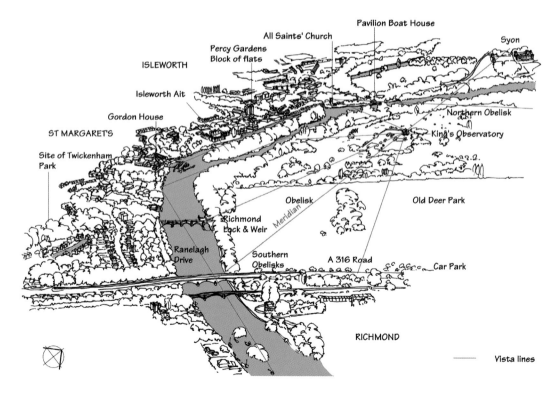

RIGHT The high points
along the Thames give
vistas that connect
Windsor Castle with
Greenwich via Richmond
Hill and St Paul's Cathedral.

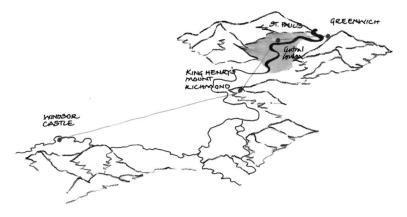

takes for an oak to reach maturity and for planning ambitions, which may seem impossible in the short term, to become realistic. Most importantly the strategy was written and illustrated in a way that made it possible for lay people to use.

Since it was published in 1994, the strategy has taken on a life of its own. Sir David Attenborough, who lives on Richmond Hill, has become its patron. All four local authorities and central government have supported and funded the strategy and employed coordinators to continue to bring everyone together to decide on priorities for this part of London through its landscape. The current coordinator, Jason Debney, has managed to galvanize enormous enthusiasm for the component projects and continues to expand the bodies that fund and support the strategy. When presented as something that makes instinctive and emotional sense, landscape is a powerful tool that allows people not only to understand their surroundings, but also to feel as though it belongs to them and that they can have an effective voice in deciding how it changes.

LONGWOOD GARDENS

PENNSYLVANIA

Across the Atlantic in Pennsylvania, I have been working with Longwood Gardens on a project to design a new entrance space to their vast sequence of glasshouses. Longwood covers over 405 hectares (1,000 acres) and is one of the premier gardens in the United States. Director Paul Redman was in the process of reviewing the long-term strategy and I proposed that, as well as creating fluidity and simplicity of movement, the new arrival space could demonstrate imaginative conservation of water and natural resources.

Longwood has nearly a million visitors a year and a rare ability to set standards of best practice over the whole continent. The gardens not only needed a dramatic outside space to complement the hectares of glass, but also a resolution to the significant level changes and the all-important popular attraction first stop – lavatory restrooms. My proposal was therefore to mould the land into a sinuous form that would sweep south to the main gardens and entrance, tucking the new building into the land.

Working with the English architect Alex Michaelis, local Philadelphia landscape architects Wells Appel and US building architects FMG, we designed a building that completely integrates into the topography. A curving spine of glass curls through the landform, creating a 185-metre (607-foot) corridor of light with top-lit domed washrooms opening off the spine. The loos are based on the design of the harem in the Topkapi Palace in Istanbul. The domed ceilings work well structurally with the insulating soil above them and the shafts of sunlight from high above bring a magical quality into the functional spaces. The corridor itself is 5 metres (16 feet) beneath the surface and the soft light on the walls is perfect for growing ferns and orchids. With the horticultural expertise of Longwood, we have created the largest green wall in North America, linking to the gardens' rainwater and

A glass-roofed corridor curves under the new landform at Longwood giving access to the underground lavatory restrooms. The corridor is lined with over 370 square metres (4,000 square feet) of ferns and orchids that provide as much oxygen as ninety trees. It is the largest green wall in North America.

greywater harvesting systems. From the conservatory, visitors enter a watery world of lush vegetation, curving down a green tunnel to a circular pool with continuous views up to the sky and forest trees above.

The project has tried to create a place that is at once functional and beautiful; playful and educational. Our aim has been to show how simple, traditional techniques of insulating buildings underground and weaving them into landscape can create great spaces simultaneously inside and outside. This really is land and architecture; and the water closets celebrate water and plants in a visible loop.

LEFT, TOP AND BOTTOM
On the northern side of the spine the lavatory domes are visible and connect to the garden service area.

RIGHT The landform curves southwards to the formal gardens, covering and insulating the lavatory complex, and visually links with the native woodland beyond.

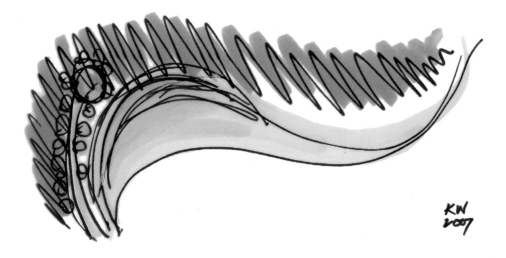

SOIL

Soil science is making great leaps. After a century of being treated as a chemical depot that can be topped up with phosphates, nitrates and potassium, soil is now being more properly perceived as a biological community of bacteria, mycorrhizal fungi and microbial life. The scientist Merlin Sheldrake has been showing how much plants depend on mycorrhizae for nutrients, water and even for communication between one another. The health of the soil and the animals and humans that live on it are intimately linked. The bacterial connections between the ground, the gut and the immune system are beginning to be better understood.

The big question is how best to revive the soils that we have exhausted over the last fifty years. Arable land that has been treated as an inert substrate for chemicals to boost crop production has proved to be a very short-term approach. Drenching farmland in artificial nitrates not only kills the organic life of the soil, it is an inefficient way of getting nutrients into plants. As more and more nitrates are needed to make the impoverished soil grow crops, the indigestible quantities are washed out into watercourses and pollute rivers and aquifers. The fragile soil, deep ploughed and no longer bound together by organic matter, also washes away into the sea. The Environment Agency estimates that across the United Kingdom two million tonnes of topsoil are eroded every year.

In the British Isles, grass grows particularly well and both protects and builds topsoil. Livestock, grazing on pasture outside rather than on corn in sheds, is an efficient method of converting photosynthesizing plants into protein, fertilizing the soil naturally and sequestering carbon back into the ground. We have to find a way of living on the land in huge numbers that works with ecological systems. The old argument runs that we can only feed the world if we pursue intensive chemical agro-industry. The new understanding of soil science suggests that we can actually only continue to produce enough food if we change our farming practices and reverse the depletion of our soil. Enclaves of special habitats must continue to be protected, but not as isolated pockets in a desert of industrial agriculture: lone Nero-like violin sonatas while the rest of the country burns. All farming needs to work harmoniously with natural systems.

VILLA LA PIETRA

FLORENCE

Villa La Pietra from the garden. The Renaissance villa and its valley above Florence have now been restored by New York University.

Stewardship of the Earth is an ideal that recurs in civilization after civilization. Virgil's poetry has become synonymous with a perfect harmony of innocent man tending the land with bucolic beasts. The Italian Renaissance drew deeply on Virgil and created a particular kind of country villa that allowed escape from the city to pure air, pure thought and physical activity.

Villa La Pietra is set in the foothills above Florence, 1.6 kilometres (1 mile) from the city gates along the ancient road to Bologna. It was initially built as the rural retreat of the Sassetti banking family in the fifteenth century. Acquired by the Capponi family in 1545 and expanded by Scipione Capponi in the seventeenth century, the villa became a classic example of an elegant country house set on a ridge overlooking the Duomo and the centre of Florence. It was flanked by walled gardens that grew olives, grapes

LEFT The seventeenth-century *limonaia* still houses the lemon trees through the winter in a pattern of horticultural expertise that has not changed in over four hundred years.

and vegetables, as well as luxuries, such as flowers and lemons. The villa was simultaneously a place of food and poetry. Decamping to the hills to escape the summer heat was part of the goal, but there was something more profound. It was felt that the city was a place of noise, corruption and commerce, where it was hard to think. Involvement with the land and plants and the sheer physical exercise of digging and pruning cleared the head for poetry and philosophy. It was a place for *otium* – peace and leisure to contemplate – as opposed to the *negotium* of the town.

In 1907 Harold Acton's mother bought Villa La Pietra and, with her husband Arthur, set about restoring the house, garden and valley to their notion of a Renaissance ideal. Together with a Florence coterie of expatriate Anglo-Americans, they had widespread influence on garden design as part of early twentieth-century country-house culture. Vita Sackville-West came to stay while she was creating the garden at Sissinghurst, as did Lawrence Johnston, the owner of Hidcote. Even Winston Churchill was a guest.

When he died in 1994, Harold Acton left the estate to New York University, who have been painstakingly restoring the place ever since. Harold particularly liked the idea of young students enjoying Florentine art and gardens and chose a university with a sufficiently deep pocket and dedication to the place to bring the villa and gardens back to health.

The restoration of the garden posed some interesting questions, such as which period to select from its long history. Apart from half of Scipione's walled garden, most of the Renaissance archaeology had been destroyed by the Incontri family when they installed a romantic 'English Garden' in the nineteenth century. Arthur and Hortense Acton, Harold's parents, then spent decades unpicking the nineteenth-century changes and creating a very individual interpretation of a formal Renaissance garden that would display their growing collection of statuary; but it was not Scipione's garden. The Acton garden reached its peak in

BELOW The restoration
of the garden has taken
fifteen years, starting
with replanting the
trees and hedges and
gradually moving on to the
crumbling stone. We have
tried to keep the wistful
magic of the place through
the rather brutal process.

the 1930s, just before the Second World War. The place was well documented
by photographs and, although by 1994 many of the structural plants had died
out, enough stumps and bumps remained to enable an accurate restoration.
The loss of the earlier layouts, the significance of the Acton garden and the
surviving evidence of its design helped to guide the decision to restore to the
1930s Acton peak.

What was more difficult was deciding how to protect the charm of the near
derelict garden, with its collapsing pavilions and toppling statues. How were we
to restore the garden without completely destroying the magic and poetry of the
place? New York University was very understanding about the proposal to take
the work gradually. Unconventionally, we felled the failing trees and hedges first,
replanting the precise lines of yew and cypress architectural structure before
tackling the crumbling walls, fountains and buildings. Somehow the memories
of the place managed to take refuge in the stone while the green architecture

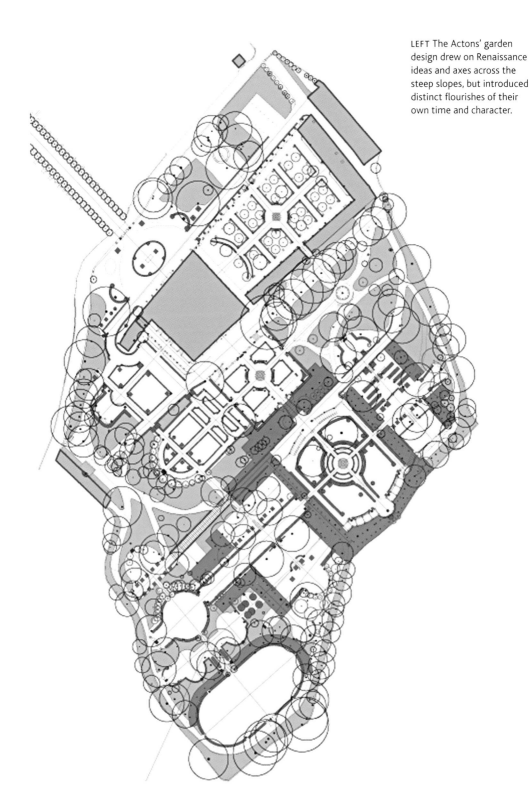

LEFT The Actons' garden design drew on Renaissance ideas and axes across the steep slopes, but introduced distinct flourishes of their own time and character.

BELOW The walled
vegetable garden survives
from the time of Scipione
Capponi and continues to
feed the villa. Fiesole can
be seen in the distance.

reassembled itself. Twenty-five years later, the garden is really coming back into
its own, with the patterns of light and shade falling sharply on crisp topiary,
while mellow stone, frogs and glow worms still capture its old poetry.

The head gardener, Nick Dakin-Elliot, has been key to the process, bringing
solid expertise on everything from drainage and foundations to pruning and
propagation. His constant presence, guidance of the gardening team and
patience with local legislation has made the restoration possible. An early
triumph was the replanting of Scipione's walled vegetable garden and the
restoration of the major collection of lemon trees in eighteenth-century
pots. Villa La Pietra is now as productive as it was in the Renaissance.

Soil conservation and productivity have been the basis of the project.
The estate straddles two sides of a 23-hectare (57-acre) valley and the main
Renaissance villa is supported by four further villas on the perimeter of the
property. These have adapted well to teaching and dormitory facilities for the
students. The central valley has now been replanted with olive groves; and a
plan for rainwater collection and greywater recycling is under consideration.
Villa La Pietra shows that the age-old concept of living sustainably on the land
can survive through changing cultures and landownerships; from a fifteenth-
century Medici banker, to a sixteenth-century cardinal, to a twentieth-
century English art dealer, to a twenty-first-century American university. The
essence and philosophy of the place have remained constant.

LEFT The long cross vista terminates in the outdoor theatre, one of the early introductions to the garden by the Actons.

RIGHT, TOP AND BOTTOM The theatre has been a place of great entertainment over the years. Margot Fonteyn, Brigitte Bardot and more recently Judi Dench and Antony Sher have all performed in the space. The box balls were planted to conceal the limelights.

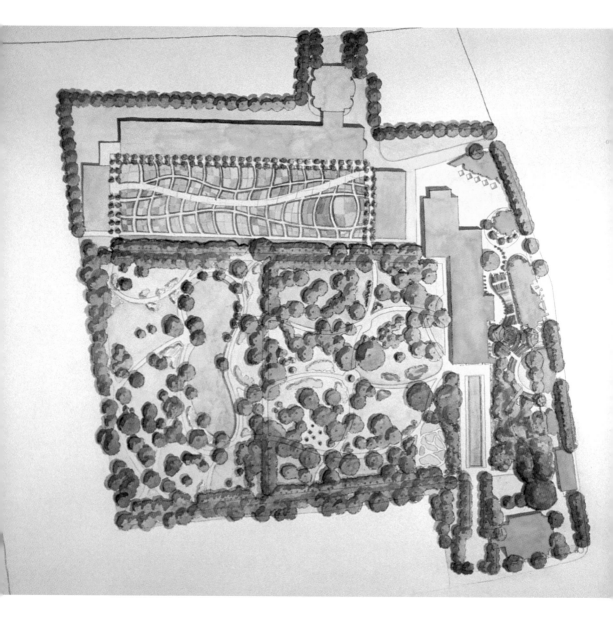

THE APOTHECARIES' GARDEN

MOSCOW

The new plan incorporates the eighteenth- and nineteenth-century layers with functional contemporary spaces that have helped to revive and reinvigorate the gardens.

The Apothecaries' Garden in Moscow shows a similar resilience and ability to adapt while still keeping its core mission and identity. In 1706 Peter the Great founded the garden as a place to raise and study medicinal plants. Peter the Great was fascinated by science and eager to bring the latest thoughts and technologies to Russia. Legend has it that Peter himself planted three of the original garden conifers with his own hands and the ancient Siberian larch, which still survives in the garden, is thought to be one of these.

The garden originally belonged to the Moscow Hospital and was then handed on to the Medical Academy. The first director of the garden, appointed in 1735, was both a doctor of medicine and a prominent botanist. By 1804, the Medical Academy had moved to the new capital, St Petersburg, and the garden was bought by Moscow University in the following year. It is interesting to follow the evolution of medical and botanical science, as well as the changing tastes in layout and design, that the garden reflects.

The early eighteenth-century orthogonal compartments of ordered physic plants, beside a rectangular reservoir to store rainwater, were gradually softened into serpentine paths, lawns, freestanding trees and a picturesque lake. By the time of Catherine the Great, later in the century, the 'English taste' had reached Russia and the garden began to resemble an urban park rather than an ordered physic garden. The emphasis and design of the garden altered with changing priorities in science, medicine, education and recreation over the centuries. The focus on plants and their display for teaching, curiosity and delight nevertheless remained. During the nineteenth century the garden became fully romantic and Chekhovian, but then Soviet re-emphasis on science returned to some taxonomic order beds and experimental plantings for analysis of food and crop varieties.

In the first hundred years, the plant collection rapidly expanded from medicinal to wider botanical and taxonomic curiosity. By 1808, Director Georg Franz Hoffmann recorded over 3,500 species in the garden. Growing plants in the extremes of Moscow heat and cold is not easy; glasshouses were essential. Political upheaval proved almost as challenging as the climate. During the 1812 Napoleonic occupation of Moscow, most of the greenhouses were destroyed, along with many plants and part of the library and herbarium. The garden recovered but had to raise funds by selling off land, reducing the area from 9 to 7.2 hectares (22 to 18 acres). Despite the Revolution, the Second World War and the Moscow University acquisition of a much larger site to the south-west, the Apothecaries' Garden somehow managed to survive as a much-loved space in the centre of a rapidly developing city.

The latest rescue of the garden is largely thanks to the cooperation of the Moscow botanist Alexei Reteyum and landscape architect Artyom Parshin, with the architect developers Sergei and Georgi Gevorkyan. Together they have brought the garden back to life, developing cafés, restaurants and offices along the street edges and restoring the crumbling glasshouses and failing collections. They invited me to draw up a masterplan for the garden in 1997. Moscow was then a very different city, just emerging into a modern economy with all its conflicting pressures.

The Apothecaries' Garden survives as one of the significant open spaces in the centre of Moscow. It is now surrounded by major buildings (BELOW LEFT), but the frame of lime avenues still encloses the garden (BELOW CENTRE).

BELOW RIGHT The garden has survived as one of the most popular public spaces in central Moscow through both summer and winter.

Working with the garden team and the architectural historian Dmitry Schvidkovsky, we agreed to restore as much of the historic layout as possible. The Chekhovian paths, lake and groves have all been saved and the original lime avenues that frame the garden are now in good health. The glasshouses have been expanded, incorporating the earlier façades, and the library has been rescued. Two new areas were incorporated as part of the masterplan – an entrance to draw people in from the south-west corner and a fresh interpretation of taxonomic order beds on a former works yard in the north east. The new entrance combines a long reflecting pool leading to the glasshouses with groups of Russian birches and pines on either side. For the works yard I proposed a grid of rectangular order beds, warped in three dimensions to accommodate changes in drainage and aspect. The works yard plans have not yet been implemented. The Russians have a deep passion for gardening, especially for fruit and vegetables, and the idea is to provide a combination of demonstration and experimental plots in a fresh and sculptural layout that still remembers the early eighteenth-century physic garden.

OXFORD BOTANIC GARDEN

OXFORD

The Oxford Botanic Garden charts a less turbulent, but in some ways parallel, history. It was founded by Sir Henry Danvers in the seventeenth century as a physic garden for 'the glorification of God and for the furtherance of learning'. The garden is set within high stone walls beside the River Cherwell and was from the start used to research the scientific and medicinal values of plants. At the end of the nineteenth century, Sir Isaac Bayley Balfour laid out rectangular botanical family borders to his adaptation of the Bentham and Hooker system of classifying plants. More recently plant classification has moved on significantly and Oxford University has successfully restored the rectangular beds and reordered them to reflect the advances in DNA fingerprinting and electron microscopy to demonstrate an evolutionary tree of life for flowering plants.

After the Second World War, the botanic garden was offered an area of Christ Church allotments beyond the walls of the seventeenth-century garden. Initially the area was developed as a display of ornamental herbaceous plants and flowering shrubs. In 2004, following our plans for the University Harcourt Arboretum, I was asked by the Oxford Botanic Garden to make proposals to rejuvenate the area.

The entrance to the Botanic Garden in Oxford,
with Magdalen tower behind.

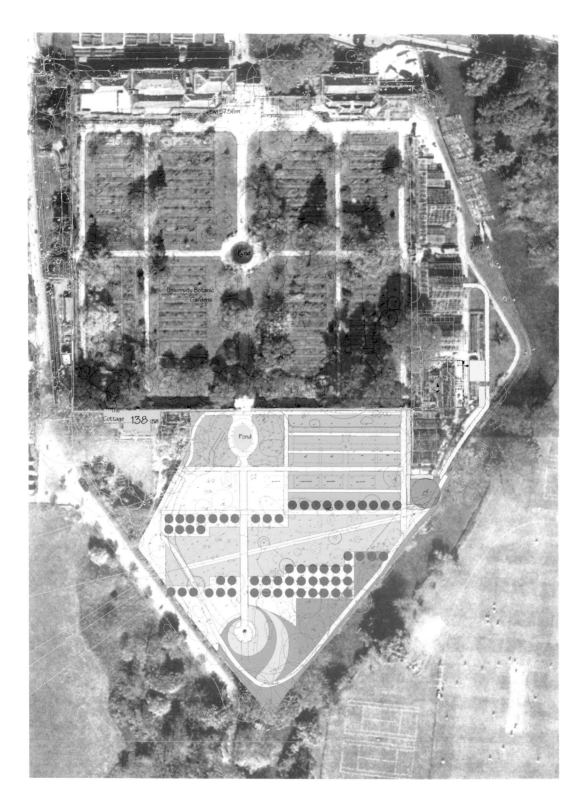

University Botanic Gardens

Pond

The Cottage 138

Pond

BM 57.56m

LEFT The new plan creates an area of fruit and vegetables beyond the seventeenth-century walls, showing how plants can be grown successfully in an urban environment to produce food and clean air and water.

BELOW The Oxford Botanic Garden is bounded by the River Cherwell and makes an ideal place to demonstrate water plants purifying and recirculating clean water.

The garden is small and perfectly formed. The position between Magdalen, Merton and Christ Church and beside the Cherwell is idyllic. Its history as the oldest botanic garden in England and the legacy of scientific thought and educational expertise is impressive. Most of all, the inner-city location by Magdalen Bridge makes the garden an easy and attractive destination for thousands of visitors a year. It reaches students, schoolchildren, Oxford residents and tourists. I discussed which message the botanic garden would most like to communicate to its broad audience. As a counterpoint to the scientific beds within the walls, and given the earlier history of the Christ Church land as allotments, I suggested that the *ultramures* area could become an elegant demonstration of inner urban sustainability – a place to show how to grow fruit and vegetables in a city and to collect and purify water using plants.

Together with the university team of Louise Allen and Piers Newth, I developed a plan to combine vegetable plots, fruit trees, and ornamental and water plants on a logical grid that related to the beds within the walls and the axial arrangement on the archway tower to Magdalen. To make the most of the space, the new layout is fractured to pick up a dramatic vista to Merton tower, creating a diagonal axis that breaks the linear pattern and helps to bring in views to the river and the centre of Oxford. The vegetables are now harvested and donated to local charities through an organization called the Oxford Food Bank.

At the same time, we spoke to the Environment Agency about making a connection to the River Cherwell and demonstrating how reed beds and filtration through water plants can cleanse the water naturally. We also worked with the sculptor Keith Wilson on initial proposals to turn the rather tired rose garden, owned by Magdalen College, at the front of the botanic garden into a new design demonstrating water collection and purification techniques, though this has not yet gone forward.

BELOW LEFT The south-facing wall and garden area beyond the historic order beds are ideal for growing food.

BELOW RIGHT The vegetables grown in the garden are distributed to local charities through the Oxford Food Bank.

LIFE

The British landscape has evolved since the last Ice Age, some ten thousand years ago, as a collaboration between humans and the natural world. It is important to understand those dynamics in order to grasp why the landscape looks the way it does and how best to conserve it. Although humans have been an intrinsic part of the environment, there is a temptation to start from an idea of pure, wild nature and an expectation that the land would be better unencumbered by mankind and would look after itself effortlessly — naturally. That rather misses the point of where we are and avoids the reality of a mushrooming population on a battered planet. We need to come up with sensible solutions rather than wish problems and humanity away. Notions of humans confined to cities and eating hydroponic food grown in skyscrapers sound like defeat. Millennia of stewardship and cooperation with natural systems should suggest better ways of tending the soil, conserving water, living with wildlife and growing healthy food. Humans have to be factored into the full spectrum of life, both as consumer and bully, with an urgent moral obligation to help manage the balance.

Dance of Death, circle of life — graffiti, Rome.

WILDLIFE

Until the industrialization of agriculture following the Second World War, European farming on the whole managed a steady balance of rotating arable crops with grazing animals in a way that kept soil, humans and wildlife healthy. Marginal land was not pushed to the limit. The ecologist Colin Tubbs, assessing his native Hampshire, believed that because of the subtle variety of farming habitats, 'the period of maximum biodiversity was around the middle of the eighteenth century rather than at some remote period'. Valuable habitats such as water meadows, heathland and coppice woodlands are essentially man-made, kept in health by constant management. In a countryside that has been shaped by agriculture and where many of our richest habitats rely on human intervention, farming sustainably is key to the survival of wildlife.

Attitudes to agriculture are buffeted by fears of starvation on the one hand and the desire for cheap food on the other. War, weather and pestilence haunt productivity. Hard as it might try, government can never quite come up with the right legislation to protect against these unpredictabilities; but then neither can an unregulated market. Agriculture cannot be treated as a purely commercial industry because too many other natural factors are at stake and the timescales are millennial. In his book *Natural Capital*, Professor Dieter Helm of New College, Oxford, makes the case for valuing long-term natural assets as part of realistic economic policy. Soil, air and water are the key assets and farming has both a need and a responsibility to look after them well. This should be directly factored into the costs of producing food, rather than surreptitiously paid for through pollution and the degradation of the environment. Farmers still need to be encouraged and supported, but in a way that recognizes all the long-term contributions to the environment that they can make.

WINCHESTER WET MEADOWS

HAMPSHIRE

The city of Winchester sits comfortably in its downland landscape. The water meadows have been protected and the cathedral remains the dominant building in the town (BELOW). The Hampshire Wildlife Trust has restored the meadows (OPPOSITE) at Winnall Moors on the northern edge of Winchester and the wild flowers and bird populations have flourished.

Rachel Carson's *Silent Spring* of 1962 helped to inform a mounting popular outrage at the destruction of habitats by industrial agriculture and urban expansion. In the justifiable fury that followed her book, it is sometimes forgotten what an important role farmers are able to play in conserving the habitats that survive. The wet meadows around Winchester are a good example. Of all the cities in England, Winchester has managed to sit particularly comfortably in its landscape. The settlement shelters in a valley bowl where the waters of the River Itchen collect. The web of streams and channels and their inherent defences helped Alfred the Great to choose the town as his capital. Marshy Winchester was reputedly the last place in Britain where you could catch malaria.

The Norman shift to London allowed Winchester to sleep on as a provincial city. Today you can still walk from the Iron Age fort in the open downland, across the medieval water meadows, through the King's Gate in the city walls and the Priory Gate to the Cathedral Close and reach the buttercross in the very centre of the city without passing a petrol station, a supermarket or a warren of retail sheds. What is more, when you look out from the buttercross, you can still see the open hillsides that surround the city and, when you approach from a distance, the towers of the cathedral, college chapel, guildhall and prison stand out as the principal buildings. Tess of the d'Urbervilles' hanging tower is the first glimpse of the city from miles away. Town and countryside remain united.

Landownership as well as topography and hydrology have helped this union to survive. The south-eastern quadrant of the city is largely owned by Winchester Cathedral and Winchester College. Between them they have combined to conserve the medieval buildings and wet landscape that stretches out to the chalk downland and the Iron Age fort. From the Middle Ages the soggy land was carefully managed as state-of-the-art medieval farming. The meadows were criss-crossed with ditches, channels and sluices

The medieval wet meadows at Winchester College are a rare habitat for birds, wild flowers and spawning salmon. Photographs and paintings from between the wars show the meadows as open and well grazed (LEFT AND BELOW). Following the economic crisis in livestock farming, grazing ceased and the meadows quickly became covered in sycamore, scrub and Japanese knotweed (RIGHT), greatly reducing the wildlife value of the land. Winchester College will now be removing the invasive species and reintroducing grazing to the meadows.

WINCHESTER

Winchester is an excellent example of a city that has stayed closely connected to its landscape. Many of the buildings are made of local flint stone; the intimate medieval streets, courtyards and closes are good places for modern life. The views and paths between the surrounding hills and the city centre have survived for over a thousand years.

that enabled the farmers to flood and drain the land, to capture warmth and fertility and gain precious weeks of early spring grass growth to fatten their sheep and cows. Technologically, the water meadows were very precise and highly advanced.

Although the intensive management of the water waned with the decline of agriculture, the meadows continued to be grazed until the 1970s. The plight of the British dairy industry then led to the removal of herds across the country and the abandonment of wet meadows from Surrey to Suffolk. Within a decade the abandoned land had sprouted trees, and a decade later meadows that had been tended and open for more than a thousand years had become thickets of poplar, sycamore, Japanese knotweed and brambles. The change to the landscape was fundamental, but because the transformation happened gradually, year by year, it largely went unnoticed. Stubble developed slowly into a full beard and people forgot that the land had ever been close shaven. Trees are seen as intrinsically good and any proposal to chop them down and revert to grazing and management as unnatural and brutal. As people are increasingly separated from an agricultural countryside, the debate develops a moral as well as a political and philosophical intensity.

Natural England, the government body responsible for the natural environment, and the Hampshire Wildlife Trust have valiantly tried to explain the wildlife significance of these wet meadows. The interaction between wild flowers, insects, birds, small mammals and fish that the gentle habitat supports is generous and complex. But the relationship between humans and wildlife has increasingly been oversimplified by a predominantly urban population into: wild good, human bad. When I proposed the felling of many of the trees on the Winchester wet meadows and the reintroduction of cattle as part of the masterplan for the college, there was growling protest from local residents. Winchester College kept its nerve and explained the history and the science of the landscape to everyone who was interested. After a series of public meetings, the consensus shifted from objection to general, and often enthusiastic, support. The adjacent grazed St Cross meadows to the south west showed how beautiful and rich in wildlife the ancient landscape could be. And to the north east, the restoration of Winnall Moors by the Hampshire Wildlife Trust demonstrated how rapidly meadows of wild flowers could be recovered. There is still discussion about how best cattle and salmon can coexist and how much stream banks can be trampled, but at least the understanding of the complex interconnections within the landscape has improved. Local people have become more connected with their environment, the delicate wildlife habitats will be saved and the views between the cathedral and the Iron Age fort will be reopened.

Conservation of healthy landscape has to look forwards. The economics of land management and the demands for food, recreation and carbon sequestration all press on the priorities and perceptions of landscape: Alexander Pope's 'use' as well as his 'genius'. Managing land well does not necessarily mean farming in a historic way or even to a historic appearance; just learning good lessons from the past that might be applicable in the future.

SHAWFORD WET MEADOWS

HAMPSHIRE

Downstream from Winchester at Shawford, the approach was very different. Between two arms of the river, 25 hectares (60 acres) of old meadow had been laser-levelled in the late twentieth century to construct a helipad and polo pitch. Both were made redundant by a change in ownership. The land is attached to a fine Carolean house and the new owners asked me to design grounds to complement the house and create a watery landscape to fit the wider environment.

Changes in layout and landownership over the centuries had erased the archaeology and relevance of earlier gardens. The sprawl of island beds and pampas grass into the wilder landscape had muddled the setting. It was time for a new design that would draw the formal gardens back around the house and release the remaining landscape back to the river. Flooding, deer and badgers urged protection for the cultivated areas, especially as a large part of the new gardens were to be laid out as vegetable parterres. The language of seventeenth-century design is strong and architectural. I was able to make an earth rampart that would wrap around the garden, linking to a new walled garden and hiding a deer fence in a sunken ditch beyond. On top of the rampart, a raised walkway gives a long view over the landscape and a corner bastion provides the lookout for an Antony Gormley 'watcher'.

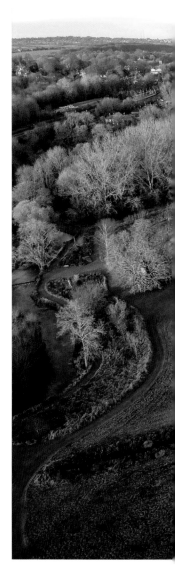

The landscape at Shawford Park is a new interpretation of a wet meadow. Curving channels have been carved down to the water table to create warm, shallow rills of alkaline water, which is the perfect habitat for the southern damselfly. Wildlife habitats can be sculptural as well as functional.

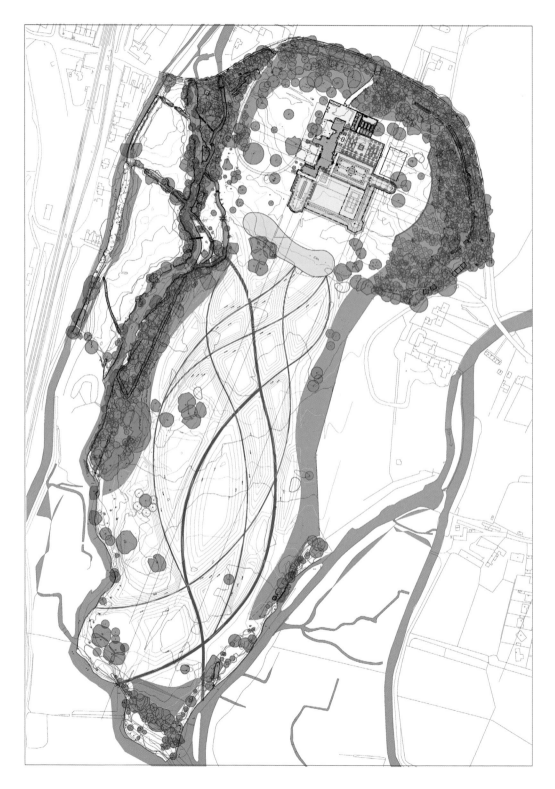

The curving channels have been designed to run from an old stew pond down to the River Itchen (LEFT). In the twentieth century the stew pond had been covered by a car park and the meadows levelled for a helipad and polo pitch. From the rampart the new quilted landform opens up (BELOW RIGHT) with mist rising from the water rills.

Beyond the rampart, the helipad and polo pitch have now been ripped out and the land parted down to the water table. The old stew pond (fish pond) has been reopened as a lake and curving channels of water course through the landscape collecting spring water to feed the river. Between the channels, the earth has been mounded up to create a sinuous quilted landscape of sheep-grazed wild flowers. On autumn evenings, the river mist rises eerily from the channels so that the woven pattern hovers in the air above. Winter frost turns the meadows into a white sculpture.

This is a completely new landform. It is neither a recreation of a water meadow nor the conjectural reconstruction of the seventeenth-century landscape. Understanding the traditions that allowed water to flow through the land and studying the native plants that used to flourish in the area helped to inform and inspire the design. Most particularly the distress of the endangered southern damselfly was key to making the space. This native turquoise dragonfly has almost become extinct as meadows have been abandoned and become covered by trees and shrubs. It depends on shallow, flowing alkaline water in full sun to feed and breed. The creation of weaving open water is exactly the habitat it needs. Both the damselfly and the otters had moved in before we had finished, blithely relaxed about the diggers and the dumpers.

Cohabitation with historic sites and fragile wildlife need not confine us to a static pattern of conservation and land management. It is critical to understand what is significant and vulnerable. But that can be a great source of inspiration for new design and fresh management, finely detailed to the site and its special peculiarities. Practical knowledge and sensitivity to the history of a place can help you leap into new territories with humour and relevance. Respect for the past and concern for wildlife can be a real stimulus for fresh ideas.

OVERLEAF In winter, frost picks out the shapes and curves and a Gormley 'watcher' observes from the new bastion in the corner of the rampart.

HEVENINGHAM HALL

SUFFOLK

On another wet meadow site in Suffolk, seventeenth-century fish ponds had silted up and become covered by alder, while the rest of the valley had been planted with tight grids of poplars. The Blyth Valley is a gentle landform with a narrow river, almost a stream, meandering down its centre. Although the valley is understated, it has some dramatic buildings on its banks. The Blyth flows past the old parish churches of Huntingfield and Walpole, which mark the western and eastern sides of the valley bowl. Huntingfield and Heveningham Halls stand to the north and south of the river. The whole landscape of trees, buildings and water had been designed to work together across the open, grazed meadows at their centre. When the meadows became filled with trees, none of the historic views and landscape relationships could be seen.

Heveningham Hall is one of those perfect eighteenth-century country houses, funded by a banking fortune and enlisting the best designers of the day. Sir Robert Taylor built the hall; James Wyatt made the interiors; and Lancelot 'Capability' Brown designed the landscape. Unfortunately Brown died the year after the design and his plans were never implemented, but he left behind an exquisite 3-metre (10-foot) watercolour drawing, which is

Heveningham Hall is a perfect eighteenth-century English country house, designed by the top architect, decorator and landscape architect of the day.

'Capability' Brown's landscape plan (BELOW) was so accurate that it could be implemented two centuries after it was drawn.

BOTTOM The Blyth Valley in 1997 with silted ponds and poplar plantations and (OPPOSITE) the valley in 2000 with the lake and parkland created to Brown's design.

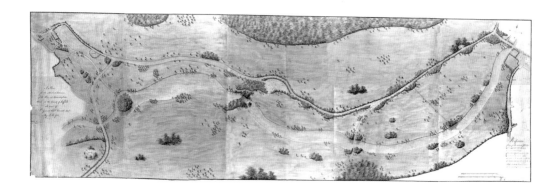

so accurate that it can be superimposed on a contemporary digital topographic survey. You can even pick out the species of the proposed trees from the precise profiles he painted. Brown's design was simple but inspired. He suggested framing the valley crest with thick, undulating woodland to give protection and definition to the estate. Parkland was to flow down from the hall and over the river, uniting both sides of the valley. The little river was to be left undisturbed, but the fish ponds beside it were to be expanded into a broad, long lake. The lake was to have the appearance of a generous river lazily curving through the landscape. The expanse of water, reflecting the sky, was designed to give the valley a scale and grandeur to complement Taylor's new mansion.

Brown's plans managed to combine simple bold gestures with finely detailed vistas. The positioning of trees and parkland clumps cleverly directed the eye away from

the centre of the valley, where the view is at its shortest and where the lake has to change level in the descending valley. It also set up symmetrical pairs of views to east and west. At opposite ends of the valley, the tower of Huntingfield church and the spire of Walpole church are framed by clumps of trees. Then, less obliquely, the vista to Huntingfield Hall was matched by a corresponding vista to an old farmhouse. Huntingfield Hall was refaced as a Gothick folly and Brown designed a classical façade for the farmhouse to resemble a Greek temple. Further upstream, Taylor also refaced the neighbouring farmhouse and Brown's plan left a hint for a future extension of the lake.

Two centuries later, Heveningham had fallen on hard times. Fires, inheritance tax and sudden death had left the place empty, with most of the land sold. After languishing on the market for several years, the house was bought in 1995 by a young family who set about restoring the landscape and the hall and gradually piecing together the original landownership. Now, almost a quarter of a century later, the estate has grown from under 200 hectares (500 acres) to over 2,225 hectares (5,500 acres). Nearly 4 kilometres (2.5 miles) of lakes have been dug and a 40-metre (130-foot) stone bridge has been built across the water, as Brown proposed. The upstream lake was completed in 2017. Roughly 340 hectares (840 acres) of grazed meadow and parkland have been created and 314 hectares (776 acres) of broadleaved native woodland planted.

The project was initially something of a conundrum for English Heritage. Although the hall is listed at Grade I and the faithful creation of a Brownian landscape surrounding the house was theoretically a good idea, the proposals could not be described as a historic restoration. The Brownian landscape had only ever existed on plan and the implementation of his designs two hundred years later would technically be a new insertion into a historic landscape. Further headaches arose with the silted fish pond that had become an alder carr of nature conservation interest. It took eighteen months of research, consultation and negotiation to agree the masterplan with all the various authorities and it will probably take another seventy-five years before the landscape comes to maturity. But the exciting thing has been that the vision of an entire estate, designed seven years before the French Revolution, still remains relevant today.

The mosaic of habitats created by the water, parkland, woodland and hedgerows is wonderfully rich in wildlife. It has transformed the bird, insect and mammal communities of this corner of Suffolk by converting miles of arable land into many different, interrelated habitats that combine native woodland edges with grazed wildflower pasture; reedy river banks with wet meadows; hedgerows with ditches; and bat-filled old buildings with stretches of insect-rich open water. Wetland birds that had been absent for decades, such as bitterns, curlews and marsh harriers, as well as litmus-test arable birds, such as cuckoos, grey partridge and plovers, have now all returned. Particularly exciting is the appearance of seventeen pairs of breeding barn owls. The place is beautiful but it is also alive.

As a social as well as landscape focus, Heveningham has also been rejuvenated. An annual fair is now held at the hall and has so far raised over £600,000 to be split between the five parishes and communities that ring the estate. Quite apart from the funds raised and the fun had, the meetings leading up to the fair each year bring the community together in a powerful and voluble way. The hall is not just the physical and architectural centre of the landscape. It has become a symbol of the local community as well.

The combination of grazed pasture, wet meadow, meandering river, open water and managed woodland create interconnected habitats that make Heveningham a haven for wildlife and a focal centre to the landscape.

NATURAL HISTORY MUSEUM

LONDON

In parallel with the revival of wildlife in farmed land and the countryside, it is also important to consider how urban areas might evolve. Changes in movement and energy storage could transform the way that cities work. As cars become electric and perhaps automated vehicles mean that private transport is largely replaced by a less wasteful shared system, then the substantial areas devoted to streets and parking can be used differently. Urban open space can be reconfigured to work with wildlife, water and food in ways that Victorian and twentieth-century towns could have hardly imagined.

London is one of the greenest cities in the world. The central thread of the Thames landscape and the generous arrangement of squares, parks and gardens make it a very good place to live. They also give the city a head start in coping with climate turbulence. But there is even more that these green spaces can do to make urban life resilient in the future and the Natural History Museum is exploring the ways. In 2014 the architect Níall McLaughlin and I won the competition to redesign the grounds with the landscape team at Peter Wilder Associates.

More than any other institution, the Natural History Museum deals with time: from the start of the solar system through to our future on Earth. With more than three hundred scientists and a collection of over 80 million specimens, it is one of the leading international bodies representing the natural world. It is also undergoing a quiet revolution. Set in 6 hectares (15 acres) of South Kensington, the museum has the largest open space along the Cromwell Road, one of the prime road arteries into London. Planning permission has now been given to revive the grounds in concert with the buildings and to make them an active part of the story.

When Alfred Waterhouse designed the main building in the 1870s, he included a careful iconography of evolution. The detailed decorations of plants and animals in the façade chart the progress from extinct species in the east to extant in the west. The grounds will now do the same. A geological wall will relate, in proportional distance, the time process from the Cambrian period (1.9 million years ago) through to the present day. Layers of stone that make up the planet's surface will be demonstrated in the wall and the corresponding plants and life that formed through each era will be represented on the land beside it. Dippy, the dinosaur skeleton that used to stand in the entrance hall, has set off for a tour around British schools. When

The entrance to the
Natural History Museum.

The detailed decorations of plants and animals in the façade chart the progress from extinct species in the east to extant in the west.

it returns, a cast of the skeleton will lunch on ferns and cycads in the east grounds, opposite the end of the Jurassic period.

At the corner of Exhibition Road and Cromwell Road, there is permission to create a completely new public square at street level, looking down over the eastern grounds. The design includes an entrance from the South Kensington Tube tunnel that would allow visitors to enter the museum grounds through a new cloister, past a primordial swamp, and into a Restaurant at the Beginning of the Universe designed by Níall McLaughlin. Budget revisions will probably result in the public square being lowered to the level of the Paleontology building, but the passage from deep time to the present should still march with the iconography of the Waterhouse building.

The western grounds by contrast look to the future. The lawns that gently descend to either side from the grand Waterhouse entrance will complement one another. While the eastern grounds trace the Earth's history back to its formation, the western half will explore where we go next and how we can continue to survive in the narrow bands of atmosphere and topsoil that make life possible in the thin biosphere of the planet. It is a vision that correlates with the science and traditions of the museum.

Britain has a long and profound relationship with the natural world. The country parson Gilbert White is given credit for beginning the study of natural history with minute daily observations of his surroundings in Selborne published in 1789. He was born at an extraordinary time, when science and philosophy were changing British attitudes to nature in a way that became intrinsic to the national cultural identity; an identity still embodied in Sir David Attenborough today.

In the western grounds, the museum will examine how natural systems, humans and wildlife are interdependent and how their mutual survival within a city can continue. London is the largest city in Europe and the Cromwell Road one of the busiest transport arteries. The aim is to show how effectively urban spaces can multitask and yet still appear calm and attractive. City parks have a lot on their shoulders. The pressures of rising temperatures and fluctuations in weather, let alone the increasing needs for human health and recreation, make these parks very important. Simultaneously they need to clean and cool the air, collect and purify rainwater, support plants and wildlife and make places that are good for city dwellers to play and relax. More than 80 per cent of the British population now lives in urban areas, and public spaces will be critical to retro-fitting cities for human survival and well-being.

At the centre of the western grounds will be a large circular dew pond. It will act as a focus for the area, providing a quiet, reflective and contemplative space teeming with wildlife. At the same time it will filter rainwater collected from the museum roof through marginal and aquatic plants. Stretching from the banks of the pond up towards the main entrance will be a long wildflower meadow. The meadow will grade from fen, through damper acid grassland to dry chalk wild flowers. The herbs and grasses will also demonstrate how green spaces can slow down and absorb the run-off from increasingly common violent storms. Surrounding the western grounds, the existing woodland vegetation will be conserved and extended to provide protection from the road. Leaves are really good at filtering the tiny pollution particles in the air that cause asthma and lung disease. The plants also automatically cool and refresh the atmosphere as it passes through their foliage. The museum will monitor and explain how the management of vegetation can transform the inner city.

Rising from the pond up to the Darwin Centre, three curving terraces will represent the natural systems of water, soil and air. They will create spaces for contemplation, education and a demonstration of the rich variety of plants that can grow well in cities, providing natural food and pollination. At the top of the path, a new maintenance and education complex will be open to the public to demonstrate the best ways of managing urban parks – from recycling green waste to making soil and keeping plants healthy. On a fragile and turbulent Earth, man and nature (through both city and countryside) need to continue evolving as collaborating colleagues rather than deadly enemies.

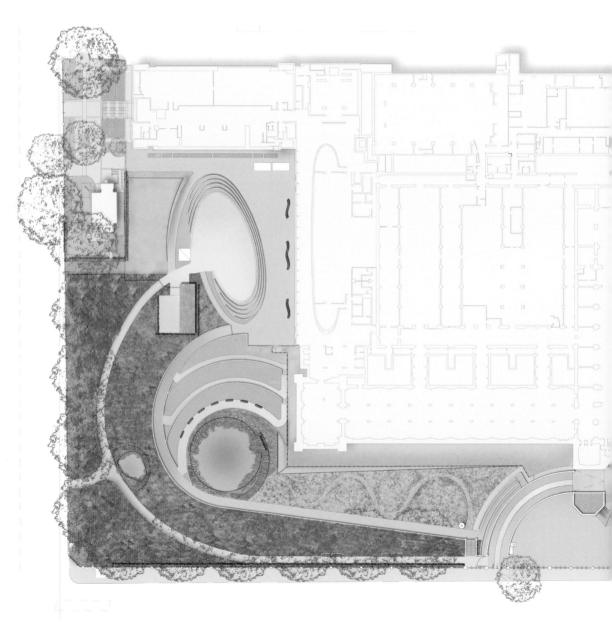

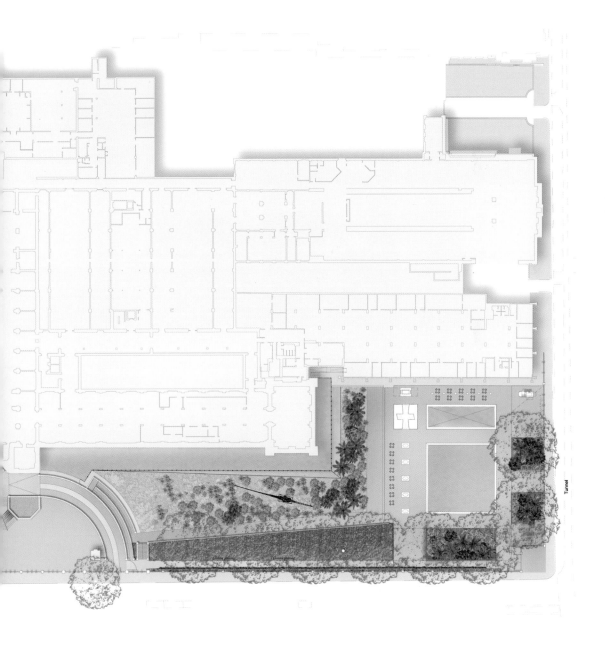

The consented plan for the grounds of the Natural History Museum, created with Níall McLaughlin and Peter Wilder.

Tunnel

RIGHT The design for the eastern grounds telling the story of geological time.

OVERLEAF The design for the western grounds showing how natural systems, humans and wildlife can survive together in the city of the future.

PEOPLE

Humans are as much a part of the landscape as wildlife. Designing spaces for busy human activity is as enjoyable and challenging as creating rich wildlife habitats and productive soil. Part of the function of urban open space is to make places for spontaneous human contact in a rushing city. The public realm should be truly democratic space where everyone feels both safe and welcome. It stretches beyond streets and parks to railway stations, churches and museums. These places have many roles and the same spot can change with time of day, season or event. Spaces such as Hyde Park and the Victoria Embankment manage to switch between relaxed deckchairs, marathons and political demonstrations. Public squares need not always be comfortable; they can sometimes inspire awe. Williams Square in Las Colinas, Dallas, is a harsh expanse of baking stone with a diagonal slash of water and bronze mustangs across the middle. It is a hostile spot, but hugely popular in the air-conditioned city for giving a sense of the land beneath its sealed protection. Whatever their character or purpose, urban spaces are always about bringing people out of their private corners to interact with the wider world.

Places for solitude and contemplation are nevertheless important too, though they are often overlooked when justification comes from quantification. Political allocation of value usually relates to numbers satisfied, but the quality of life is hard to reduce to numbers. I have been struck by the public spaces that open up briefly on the foreshore of the Thames between tides. Beaches and walks along gravel spits allow people to walk alone peacefully beside the water and forget for a moment that they are in the middle of a huge metropolis. Urban sanity may depend on time to wander and ponder on your own.

VICTORIA AND ALBERT MUSEUM

LONDON

The Victoria and Albert Museum has one of the best collections of art and design in the world, with more than 4.5 million treasures. You can wander for days, constantly surprised by the variety of the collections, from iron cemetery crosses to the latest contemporary designs of glass. Although one of the pleasures of the place is to become lost in the labyrinth and be endlessly amazed by the eccentricity and beauty of human art and imagination, the museum is aiming to become more accessible and approachable.

The FuturePlan for the V&A covers a complex of buildings over 5 hectares (12.5 acres) in south-west London. At the centre of the site is a courtyard garden that brings light and a fulcrum of orientation into the heart of the museum. When the museum was first laid out by Francis Fowke in 1852, This courtyard was the main entrance, designed as a grand Italianate façade, set back 100 metres (360 feet) from the Cromwell Road. As the museum grew and new galleries were built, the grand entrance was cut off from the road by a new southern wing designed by Aston Webb in 1899. This resulted in a much smaller space (60 x 40 metres/216 x 144 feet) that sits beneath a super-confident façade, originally designed to be viewed from a distance.

Comfortable solitude in the city is as precious as gathering spaces. The foreshore that opens up at Chiswick Mall in London (LEFT) allows people to stroll along the gravel banks, surrounded by water while the tide is out. At the Victoria and Albert Museum, not far away (RIGHT), visitors can paddle in the reflecting pond in the centre of the museum.

The style and scale of the architecture disconcerted some people, and the courtyard garden has been through a few permutations. A garden of cherry trees was replaced by dense plantings of alders and incense cedars, aimed to damp down the architecture. The combination of deep shade from the trees and dark film on the museum windows against ultraviolet light meant that many visitors passed by without even being aware of the courtyard. The FuturePlan aimed to change all this and turn the garden into the pivotal space at the centre of the museum. A single donation from the entrepreneur and philanthropist Sir John Madejski made the project possible.

In 2005 the V&A held an international competition for a new courtyard garden. The competition came with a brief that simultaneously made complete sense and yet seemed impossible to achieve. The museum wanted a green and intimate garden where two people would feel relaxed and comfortable – so far so good; that would be flexible for displays, events, cafés and fairs – tricky; that could instantly transform into a performance space for two thousand and then turn back into a gentle garden again – a challenge. The space is small, the architecture is big and the uses gloriously unpredictable.

My practice won the competition, proposing water as the solution. Rather than hide the façade behind mounding and trees, the idea was to open up and reveal the architecture. Digging down allows the former entrance once more to be approached up steps from the pond, giving the building back its feet and ankles. And creating an expanse of reflecting water bounces in light and doubles the sense of space. Most importantly for the use of the courtyard, the water is shallow and can be drained away to a tank in less than an hour, creating a large stone performance space. So the garden can indeed metamorphose from a tranquil oasis of grass and water into an intense gathering for two thousand or more and then back again within an afternoon.

Constructing that space in less than six months was a whole further challenge. Extracting tonnes of spoil from an internal courtyard, through a museum stuffed with delicate treasures and people, was not easy.

BELOW AND OVERLEAF The Victoria and Albert Museum courtyard garden with an elliptical reflecting pool that brings light and movement into the space. The pool can be drained in less than an hour to create a performance space for a couple of thousand people.

The first thought was to crane everything out over the roofs, but it quickly became apparent that temporarily reinforcing the roofs, in case a tonne load fell off the crane, was going to be more expensive than the rest of the project put together. In the end we opted for thirty wheelbarrows with thirty very fit Ukrainians. In an age of computerized mechanization, the power of human muscle should not be underestimated. We opened on time – just – on 5 July 2005.

The V&A has been wonderfully relaxed about letting people use the space. You are allowed to lie on the grass, paddle in the water and move the chairs around wherever you choose to sit. The result has been to create a truly flexible garden, protected from noise and traffic, with a warm microclimate right in the heart of Museumland. Visitor numbers have not only increased, but also diversified across age and cultures. Many more young people and children now come to the museum, attracted by the garden. Some of them may not even visit the exhibits, but with the logic of the Jesuits, if you can persuade people to come in through the great doors as young children, the chances of them returning to explore as adults are greatly enhanced.

The V&A has also refurbished the gallery along the southern side as a space for sculpture, so the doors can now open to a café terrace and the dark film be peeled off the windows. In combination with the new restaurant

OPPOSITE AND BELOW
The V&A garden has a special microclimate that enables tender plants such as *Echium pininana* and *Geranium maderense* to grow. Fountains echo the form of the planting. At night the space is used for special events. Glass planters were designed to glow like ice cubes and Patrick Woodroffe lit the building to emphasize the depth and detail of the window reveals.

on the north side, the whole courtyard zone becomes a welcoming fulcrum. At night it turns into yet another kind of space. I worked with the lighting designer Patrick Woodroffe to make the garden a dramatic place for evening events. Rather than wash the walls with uplights, he introduced special Italian fixtures designed to illuminate the surrounds of each window, giving the building an extraordinary depth and life. I have had a long fascination with glass and managed to design planters as cubes of glass that were lit from beneath, looking like lumps of glacial ice around the reflecting water. Inevitably, gardens change and the glass planters and lemon trees have since been replaced by blob-pruned trees in black boxes.

The microclimate makes the courtyard a great place for plants. *Echium pininana*, *Salvia guaranitica*, *Geranium maderense* and *Agapanthus africanus* all thrive within the walls, when they have been wiped out by severe winters elsewhere. Rich-blue hydrangeas cope with the shade along the sides and lemon trees used to sit in the glass planters to be replaced by bay obelisks in the winter. The planting has to be strong to hold its own against the architecture, but the palette is rich and enjoyable. Over the years different regimes have changed some of the planting and planters, but the spirit of the garden remains. *Time Out* featured it as one of the top four places in London for proposals of marriage.

In summer the glass cubes were planted with lemon trees, and *Iris pallida* var. *dalmatica* under the liquidambar trees provided fresh colour and sculptural leaves.

This is a space where the design has deliberately acted as a foil for the people, the activity and the Grade I architecture. The layout quietly complies with the strong symmetry of the building. The dark red sandstone and creamy York stone echo the colours of the Victorian brick and pale terracotta. The trees frame rather than mask the façade and the southern café terrace works with the sculpture gallery. But at the same time as being courteous to its setting and uses, I hope that the space feels like a strong statement of its own time. The form of the ellipse of steps and ramps is sculptural and far from Victorian. The glass planters and lighting were made to be unexpected and dramatic. The water is functional and playful. Design based on use and context can be understated and respectful while still retaining strength and identity.

HYDE PARK CORNER

LONDON

Just up the road at Hyde Park Corner, I tried the same approach – gently but stubbornly working at the need for contemporary movement across London while respecting the historic context. The challenge was to turn a nightmare of a traffic roundabout into a space that could connect the royal parks and be enjoyed by people on foot, horseback and bicycle.

Hyde Park Corner is the major vehicle junction in the weaving chaos of London streets. It has always been a fulcrum of motion, albeit rather idiosyncratic and eccentric. London is different in form, politics and character from its continental counterparts. It is not a city of baroque, axial boulevards and does not have the rectilinear, military organization of the Champs Elysées or Unter den Linden. London actually feels rather anarchic. It has evolved more around the natural features of parks, the river and the oddities of private landownership than from the disciplines of defence and political ideology.

A Saxon trackway from Charing Cross used to run through Piccadilly along the dry ground above the level cut in the river banks at times of high flood. The track gradually evolved into the main London road to the west. Perched on the top of this first Thames flood terrace, Hyde Park Corner is right on this western route in and out of the city. It was the toll gate for the road leaving

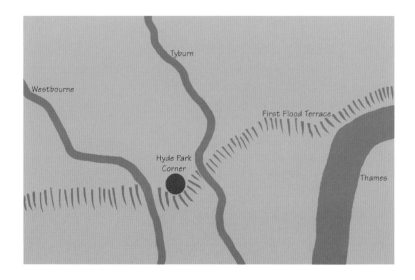

OPPOSITE AND BELOW Hyde Park Corner sits at a critical nexus of routes into London from the west. It has become a symbolic space celebrating the transition from war to peace, from Empire to Commonwealth and from royal enclosure to popular landscape. The New Zealand War Memorial, opened in 2006, completes the north-eastern side of the space.

London at the crossing between the Westbourne and Tyburn tributaries and became the pivot of the wonderfully crooked processional route linking the royal palaces through the royal parks. In character with the capital, this fulcrum is in essence a green space rather than an urban plaza. The arch at the centre looks more like an ornament in a landscape park than the Arc de Triomphe or the Brandenburger Tor, and the symbolism is more to do with peace than war. The very nature of the ceremonial dog-leg at Hyde Park

LEFT The Hyde Park Corner Royal Artillery Memorial by Charles Sargeant Jagger is deeply moving, capturing the human devastation of the First World War.

RIGHT, TOP Hyde Park Corner remains one of the great junctions of London, but now pedestrians and horses are able to cross and enjoy the space protected from vehicles.

RIGHT, BOTTOM Symbolically, the Wellington Arch is surmounted by a statue of Peace vanquishing War; there is no triumphalism.

Corner is symbolic. It is not just a physical change of direction. It represents a change of attitude from war to peace; from Empire to Commonwealth; and from royal enclosure to popular landscape.

Although Hyde Park Corner is the crucial link in the sequence of public open spaces right across London, 1960s road engineering and a maze of intimidating subways did not encourage people through the area. The crude curve of asphalt around the Wellington Arch and the confusion of underground passages were hostile to anyone not in a vehicle. Everything had been designed for the car.

Landownership in London is complicated. Over the centuries, responsibility for the administration and maintenance of royal lands has been gradually transferred to various government bodies through a series of intricate acts. Hyde Park Corner falls between the tectonic plates of the Crown Estate, the Department for Digital, Culture, Media and Sport, Westminster City Council, Transport for London, the Royal Parks, the Greater London Authority, English Heritage and London Underground, among others. In 2000 English Heritage, who had taken over responsibility for the Wellington Arch, rather bravely set up a steering committee to do something about Hyde Park Corner and put the project out to competition.

There have probably been as many *grands projets* suggested for Hyde Park Corner as Trafalgar Square. Robert Adam made designs for the area in 1778, Aston Webb proposed a new processional route in 1901 and Edwin Lutyens came up with a plan for a vast formal plaza at the intersection in 1937. But there seems to be a national allergy to monumental urban statements. Although the Mall and Constitution Hill have been formalized, the general incremental and haphazard way that the city has evolved is part of its charm and its success. English Heritage recognized three very important things: that there was no money; that the grander the *projet*, the less likely the support; and that a coordinated sequence of short- and long-term projects would be more practical and achievable than a single assault.

The Royal Parks Review, chaired by Dame Jennifer Jenkins with Sir Terry Farrell, had already achieved a major breakthrough by allowing pedestrians to

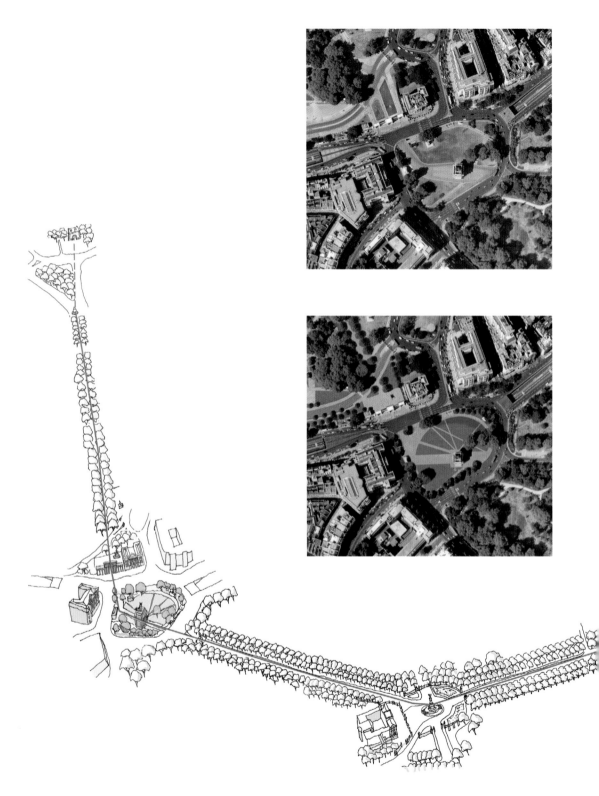

LEFT Hyde Park Corner is a fulcrum in the typically eccentric ceremonial dog-leg of London. The space, which used to be dominated by vehicles and traffic layouts (TOP), has now been softened to create a green pedestrian place linking the Royal Parks and memorializing peace (BOTTOM).

cross over to the space on the surface rather than in underground subways. Having won the competition to redesign the space, my proposal was to extend this principle, making the place welcoming to pedestrians and horses, while still allowing cars and buses to flow around the perimeter. The first step was to remove the 1960s road layout, open the gates through the arch on the ceremonial route and fill in the subway to Green Park. The second step was to make a space where people would like to linger: a peaceful eddy off a strong flow. Although besieged by traffic, Hyde Park Corner actually has an unexpected number of intrinsic advantages. It is a nexus between open spaces with its own Tube station very close to the surface. It lies on a pronounced south-west-facing slope, with excellent afternoon and evening sun. And it has the most moving war memorials in London.

Apart from inaccessibility, the problem has always been noise, pollution and the dominance of traffic. The space is surprisingly generous – over 1.5 hectares (3.7 acres) – and the proposal was to screen out the vehicles and modify the landform to help create a comfortable place to meet and linger. To the south-west I proposed building a curving water wall to hold the space and block out the traffic from Victoria. To the north-east, I suggested raising the land in a gentle grass bank. These have now been achieved. The last main elements left to complete are the sculpting of the central space to create a more receptive concave landform; the creation of a new parade ground south of Apsley House, relocating the mounted statue of Wellington to its centre; and opening the Tube station out into a café and restaurant to encourage people to eat and relax in the space.

Consultation with the authorities and local groups is an essential part of

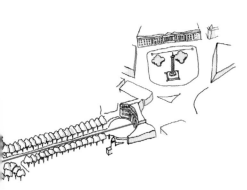

a project of this complexity that lasts over decades. Equally, where there is no money, as is often the case with public projects, you have to be imaginative with thoughts on funding. This is not always acknowledged as the responsibility of the designer, but I have found that where you want to make major changes in the public realm you have to become involved in politics, finance and inventive lobbying. This was certainly the case with the Thames Landscape Strategy. At Hyde Park Corner, Philip Davies of English Heritage and I approached the Australian and New Zealand High Commissioners, who were looking for sites for war memorials, and proposed that Hyde Park Corner might be an appropriate location. The coincidence of ambitions for the space made the projects possible.

Hyde Park Corner still has a way to go, but it is already a more comfortable and popular place than it was in 2000. The project really brought home to me how relatively small incremental changes within the flow of the possible can make real differences to urban life. The big gesture is not always necessary, possible or even desirable.

HYDE ABBEY GARDEN

WINCHESTER

At a much smaller scale, a new park in Winchester has managed a similar reconciliation between history, movement and gathering. The park was made on the site of a twelfth-century Benedictine monastery at Hyde. The abbey was built just outside the city walls and almost rivalled the cathedral in scale and wealth.

Winchester was the royal city of Alfred the Great but the bones of the king, who founded the city in 880 AD, were peripatetic. Alfred was buried in the Old Minster of Winchester in 889, then was moved to the New Minster in 903, then moved again in 1110 with his wife Ealhswith and his son Edward the Elder to Hyde Abbey, and was then rudely disinterred after the cultural revolution of Henry VIII levelled Hyde Abbey church. The site disappeared under prison grounds and was later converted to a municipal car park.

The ruins of one of the great sacred places in England had been all but forgotten under the cars, until excavations in 1999 revealed the foundations of the church and the empty graves of Alfred and his family. The local residents took a keen interest in the excavations and then lobbied Winchester Museum Service to keep the site open rather than return the area to car parking. Winchester City Council then came together with the residents to agree a competition for the removal of cars and creation of a new park linking Hyde back to the cathedral. I won the competition with a simple plan that remembered the church beneath the ground and opened the space for people to use.

The glass panel of Hyde Abbey church by Tracey Sheppard shows the final resting place of Alfred the Great. A garden has been carved out of a municipal car park and created over the ruins of the church. The columns and ledger stones in the glass panel line up with the features in the garden to help people imagine the lost building that the space commemorates.

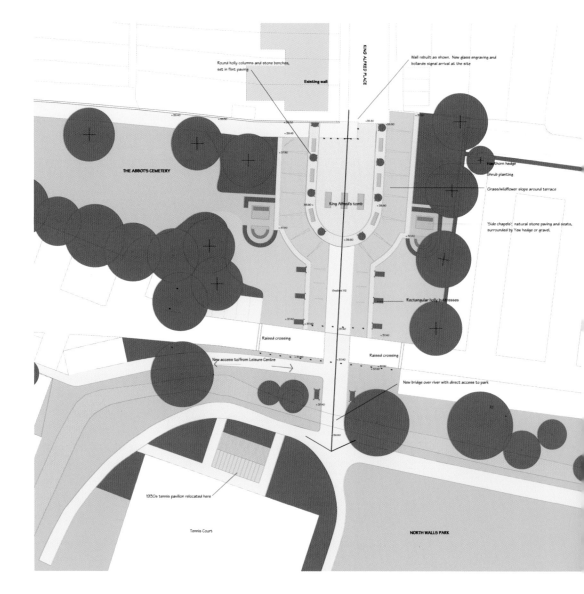

The former car park (FAR LEFT) hid the remains of the sacred site and local residents combined with Winchester City Council to create a small garden where residents can pause and sit on a new link across the city (LEFT AND BELOW LEFT). Cylinders of holly, girded with steel, mark the positions of the Saxon church columns (BELOW RIGHT).

KEY

Trees (existing/proposed)

Hedge, shrubs, herbaceous

Short mown grass

Wildflower/ longer grass/bulbs

Self binding gravel (e.g. Breedon gravel)

Bound gravel (bitmac with bonded gravel wearing course)

Flint paving

Natural stone (incl. riven slate tomb stones)

Stainless steel bollards

Timber benches (straight & curved)

Buildings

Holly columns in steel frames, with lighting attached (glass cylinders)

The whole project was made possible by the relentless energy of a remarkable local resident. Barbara Hall set up the Friends of Hyde Abbey Garden and devoted more than five years of her life to getting the project approved, funded and built. Local authority car parks are gold dust. They bring in good revenue and demand for parking in city centres is insatiable. So to give up car space to help fund a park and to allow local residents to take over an area of public land is a brave departure for a local authority. Hyde Abbey Garden is testimony to how collaboration between a local community and its government can work.

The design for the park is deliberately uncomplicated and easy to maintain. The ruins of the abbey church are picked out as a modern garden of flint, gravel and stone above the foundations. Native plantings of oak, hazel and yew frame the space and great cylinders of holly, girded with stainless steel, repeat the positions of the church columns. The memory of the church can be glimpsed through a glass panel created by Tracey Sheppard, a glass engraver and local resident. The glass panel superimposes an impression of the twelfth-century church on the holly columns and layout of the foundations. Oak benches are inspired by seats in the cathedral and extend to create an axial bridge over the river. Huge ledger stones mark the graves of Alfred and his family.

The little park has become a focus for the neighbourhood and a popular gathering place on the path to the centre of the city. Because the funding, construction, planting and now the ongoing maintenance have in large part been undertaken by local residents, there is a strong sense of ownership and pride in the place. When vandals smashed the glass panel in 2010, local donations were raised in record time to make and engrave a replacement.

MAGGIE'S CENTRE

SWANSEA

Community gardens have a unique ability to bring people together, especially where it involves active participation in allotment or productive gardens. The focus on a love of growing plants manages to cross lines of wealth, age and cultural divide. Gardens are also great for helping grief and disorientation.

Maggie Keswick, before she died of cancer in 1995, started a charity to build cancer advice centres attached to hospitals around the United Kingdom. Her husband, Charles Jencks, has ever since been passionate in support of these centres. Maggie's Centres are places where you can go to understand treatment and meet people facing similar issues. Maggie, and then Charles, set out to create buildings and spaces that were beautifully designed to welcome people with warmth and dignity.

The new vegetable garden being laid out for the Swansea Maggie's Centre.

LEFT The landscape was designed to swirl around the Kisho Kurokawa building, creating spaces for people to gather together or quietly sit alone.

ABOVE The maturing vegetable garden where visitors can work with one another and enjoy the produce.

In the grounds of the Singleton Hospital in Swansea, the Japanese architect Kisho Kurokawa, a close friend of Charles Jencks, designed a dynamic building just before he died. I was asked to place the building in its landscape and create the garden setting. The comet-like shape of the building suggested a swirling form where the landscape spins off the structure. On the eastern approach up from the main hospital buildings, visitors enter through a vegetable garden to a terrace where they can sit in the sun and shell peas and beans. Out to the west there is a calmer meadow, enclosed by a curving dry-stone wall. A mown grass path meanders through wild flowers. The enclosing wall descends to a curved bench around a quiet lawn with a view south out to Swansea Bay. Ed Coveney built the stone wall and Terra Firma worked as executive landscape architects on the gardens.

CITY OF LONDON CEMETERY

LONDON

Although we tend to think of social spaces in terms of urban squares or public parks, cemeteries are another kind of important community landscape. Not only are they places where strangers are brought together in a common mood of grieving and remembering. They are also the places for a continuing relationship with the dead, or at least our vibrant memories of them; another kind of community that we have become clumsy at dealing with.

One of my more unusual commissions was for the City of London Cemetery. By 1856 the city had run out of burial space in central London and there were concerns for hygiene and sanitation within the confines of its crowded 106 parishes. It was decided to make a new cemetery on land at Manor Park in the East End of London. A hundred and fifty years later, this cemetery too is running out of space and my brief was wonderfully brief: 'Design a way to bury the dead in the coming century that is sustainable in terms of space, energy, dignity and financial viability.'

The City of London Cemetery now covers 81 hectares (200 acres) of well-tended trees, lawns and shrubberies, but there is a hidden corner that has been used as a rubbish tip for nearly a century, gradually growing higher and spreading wider. The tip is tucked behind trees and banks and has served a useful function, but with advances in recycling, not to mention pressure on burial space, it is something of a wasted asset.

The City of London Cemetery at Manor Park.

LEFT The green waste site for the new burial ground.

BELOW RIGHT The nineteenth-century catacombs immediately to the north of the site.

The City of London Corporation has been very advanced in its attitude to death. It built the first crematorium in Greater London in 1902 and welcomes all denominations and burial methods, including catacombs (where coffins are placed on shelves above one another) and columbaria (where cremation urns are stacked). As space becomes more limited and populations increase, the corporation is open to new ideas for dealing with our dead. One of the problems is that cemeteries are very expensive to maintain and, by their nature, the people who funded their graves are no longer around when the stones begin to collapse in a rather mobile soil a few decades later.

The unusual character of this green-waste site called for an unorthodox solution. Traditional graves or tombstones would not work in such an unstable, inappropriate soil, but the raised ground surrounded by tall trees suggested that a landform solution might work. At the same time, I was taken by the dual nature of a cemetery. On the one hand, it is a place for solitary contemplation of eternity; on the other, it is an area where the dead are laid out together in space-efficient patterns not dissimilar from town plans. We take our urban layouts with us to the grave to create strikingly similar neighbourhoods in death – and probably complain just as much about the designs and ornamentations of our neighbours. Medieval churchyards have a dense and organic pattern that resembles their villages. The cemetery of Père Lachaise in Paris was deliberately laid out like elegant Parisian streets. Lawn and woodland cemeteries mirror the Anglo-Saxon desire for garden and sylvan suburbs. How do we think about our cities for the dead and the living in the coming century?

Carbon and recycling are pressing issues. Cremation solves the problem of space but requires intense energy and for some religions flames have uncomfortable associations with hell fire. The Romans understood how quickly and cleanly a dead body will decompose if it is not sealed away. Catacombs and ossuaries (where the bones from the catacombs were later assembled together) were highly effective ways of dealing with lack of space and low-energy requirements. They also form stable structures that do not require intense maintenance to cope with subsidence. The problem was how to create a burial ground that worked in such an efficient, simple and sustainable way that also spoke to the English love of space, greenery and contemplation of nature.

After a great deal of research and advice from the excellent engineers Integral, I proposed reforming the long, curving space into a landscape of rolling grass mounds which ripple down across the site, surrounded by an elevated terrace walk. The dip slopes of the rolling mounds are continuously grassy while the scarps are vertical faces of slate and stone, giving access to the burial chambers. Looking out eastwards from the high point of the cemetery, all you will see is undulating grass stretching down to the Wanstead flats. Approaching from the east, a series of curving stone faces will lead you to each tomb. Catacombs, columbaria and crypts will be built into the mounds. The boundary will be defined by ramparts that also rise and fall. The top will be broad enough to accommodate a path and standing memorials. The idea draws on the Orkney long barrows and the sacred landscape of Salisbury Plain with its distant perspectives over simple grass and sky, punctuated by burial mounds and standing stones.

The Director of the City of London Cemetery, Ian Hussein, was amazingly imaginative and receptive to these unorthodox ideas for the new burial ground. With all the earth moving and structural work for the mounds and tombs, the capital investment is nevertheless daunting and the project has not yet started.

BELOW The proposed new burial mounds inspired by the Orkney long barrows that will house catacombs, columbaria and crypts.

RIGHT The burial mounds wind down through the site, flanked by descending ramparts. From the south visitors will look out over a field of rippling wild flowers with the curving stone faces of the mounds approached from the north east.

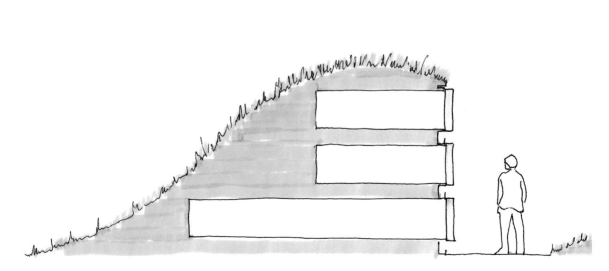

SETTLEMENT

More recently I have turned from the dead to the living. The pressures for new housing and the speed of change in urban life and technology make new settlements particularly interesting. The movement of people on foot and bicycles is starting to take priority over vehicles. New delivery and transport systems could make vast surface car parking a thing of the past, releasing large areas of urban land for new open ground. And as cities get higher and denser, the relationship between dwelling and private outdoor space becomes more precious. The use of land altogether is more thoughtful. Every square metre has to count and the integration with displaced productive farmland is increasingly pertinent. Public open space is turning richer and more complex. It has to deliver more than ornamentation or recreation; it must also work with natural systems of drainage, air quality and wildlife habitat, in addition to the demands to grow perishable food close to where people live. This affects retro-fits of existing cities as well as new settlements.

Land uses and priorities are certainly changing with the technology, and planning has some influence, but ultimately it is land values that determine how and where redevelopment occurs. Three different projects show new settlements in very different places, but with strong economic and environmental imperatives: an old established city quarter in London; a redundant industrial site on Southampton Water; and open, uninhabited desert in Oman. The redevelopment of Chelsea Barracks became possible because urban security is no longer best achieved by stationing large numbers of soldiers within a city. Fawley Waterside will replace a redundant oil-fired power station. And the new city in Oman is responding to commercial and housing pressures in the narrow belt of land between the sea and mountains west of Muscat.

CHELSEA BARRACKS

LONDON

The masterplan is laid out as a series of London squares that integrate with the surrounding urban pattern and encourage people to walk through and use the spaces.

The Chelsea Barracks project is unusual for the scale of redevelopment within the centre of an existing city. The site covers 5.2 hectares (12.8 acres) in central London. The scale, location, level of investment and commitment to long-term management in this site made it possible to consider a way of living that could help to set a new pattern.

From the outset the development has been planned around the spaces rather than the buildings. A detailed planning application for the landscape and public realm was approved in 2011 but the various building envelopes were limited to outline parameters. The project is now being built out by

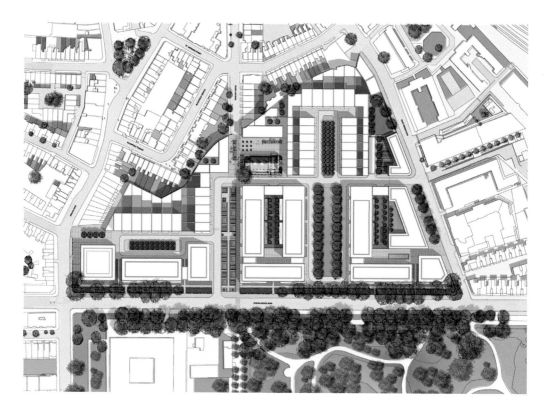

a range of architects who are refining and detailing the masterplan that I designed with Michael Squire and Dixon Jones.

In the nineteenth century, a big section of Chelsea had been fenced off to build the military barracks, blocking and severing former street patterns. A central aim of the masterplan was to reopen these old routes across the area. The guiding principle was to make the place as welcoming as possible and to encourage the public to walk through the repaired connections. Streets, squares, shops, cafés and sports, cultural and health facilities were to link the new houses back into the neighbourhood. The old Garrison Square was set as the physical and social centre of the development with the refurbished chapel in a focal role as a place for music, art, display and gatherings. It was hoped that the Orange Square farmers' market would use the square on Saturdays.

The landscape concept was to work with the traditional pattern of London squares and create a variety of public spaces inspired by the stewardship of soil, water and air. As well as offering play and recreation, the open spaces will capture rainwater, filter air, compost waste, nourish wildlife and even grow food. Historically, the combination of deep and well-watered soils on what used to be the edge of London made Chelsea a prime place for growing fruit and vegetables to feed the capital. The healthy position upstream and

BELOW The redevelopment of the Chelsea Barracks site in London comes at a turning point in our attitude to cities and the environment. The landscape concept is to create a sequence of squares and gardens that are inspired by the stewardship of soil, air and water.

OPPOSITE The old Garrison Chapel survives at the centre of the site and is planned to become a focus for art, music and a weekly farmers' market linked to the adjacent productive garden.

upwind of central London, together with speedy connections along the river, turned the area into a popular place to live for people like Sir Thomas More (resident at Beaufort House 1520–35) and a prime location for the Royal Hospital (founded by Charles II in 1681). The fashionable suburban idyll was protected and perpetuated by the residential squares developed by the Grosvenor and Cadogan estates in the eighteenth and nineteenth centuries.

London squares create an excellent template for productive and sustainable open spaces. While they provide a familiar and comfortable format of green rectangles lined by trees and protected by railings, squares are also extraordinarily adaptable in terms of use and planting. The centrepiece of the axial entrance to the new neighbourhood was designed as a 100-metre (328-foot) long productive garden. As a clear statement about the character and philosophy of the development, an immaculately tended herb, fruit and vegetable garden would lead up to the central square, with its farmers' market and destination restaurant.

Although the scheme has now moved on from the consented masterplan, the original garden was designed to be lush and sculptural in the way that the gardens of vegetables at Château de Villandry in the Loire manage to look as polished as any parterre. Yet at the same time, the garden was intended to

LEFT The Bourne Walk along Chelsea Bridge Road remembers the Westbourne River that used to flow through the site.

BELOW The restaurant designed by Ben Pentreath at the head of the central vegetable garden.

be vigorously managed to grow vegetables, herbs and salads for sale in the restaurant and market, demonstrating that it is both practical and beautiful to grow perishable food in the centre of cities. I worked with Sarah Raven to come up with a rotation of salads and vegetables to succeed commercially as well as look attractive throughout the year. Polished green, purple and ochre masonry was envisaged in a grid of 6-metre (20-foot) square raised planters, underlit with bright colours. A central pedestrian path, lined by narrow, lit rills of fast-moving water, was designed to circulate rainwater harvested from the new neighbourhood. Sculptural stainless steel Archimedes screws would raise the water from the rills to irrigate the beds. Contemporary glasshouses were to be built in the centre of the garden to grow seedlings for the productive beds. Basal heat from the mechanical and engineering plant beneath the garden was planned to keep plants growing vigorously throughout the winter.

At its heart, the Chelsea Barracks development aimed to show that even in the richest international neighbourhoods, growing food and harvesting natural resources can be an integral and welcomed part of design. Urban farming is not just for Detroit wastelands or Havana deprivation: it can form a sensible and acceptable part of every development.

FAWLEY WATERSIDE

HAMPSHIRE

Fawley Power Station was commissioned on the edge of Southampton Water in 1971. The structure was boldly designed with tessellated-glass upper storeys and a control room suspended out towards the water like a flying saucer. A dock opened straight from the building to the sea. The power station made use of the adjacent oil refinery to burn heavy fuel oil and was directly connected to the National Grid. In many ways Fawley represented the best technology and design optimism of Britain emerging from the Second World War. Forty years later, the brave new power station was condemned as inefficient, polluting and in contravention of the European Union Large Combustion Plants Directive. It was shut down in 2013.

Fawley Power Station and the oil refinery are located on a wild stretch of land on the south-eastern edge of the New Forest beside the Solent. The land formed part of the Cadland Estate, owned by the Drummond family since 1772. A third of the estate was compulsorily purchased in 1947 for the oil refinery. The construction of the refinery, now the largest in the United

BELOW LEFT The 1971 power station at Fawley.

BELOW The beautiful tessellated glass that lit the turbine hall.

Kingdom, involved the demolition of the family mansion, designed by Henry Holland and set in a 'Capability' Brown landscape. The rest of Cadland is still owned by the Drummonds and Aldred Drummond has now managed to buy back the power station site to link the land again into the estate.

The repair and reuse of this brownfield site touches on many pivotal issues of our time. The building is dramatic and represents a bold twentieth-century vision; a vision now condemned as profoundly environmentally destructive. The site occupies a critical zone between the New Forest and the coastal estuary, both internationally rare and protected habitats. In a perfect world the power station might return to its former wild and farmed state, but it will take millions of pounds to demolish the redundant structures and to make the land safe. The south coast of England is under intense pressure for housing, Southampton has become one of the largest ports in Britain and the brownfield site, with its dock and connection to the sea, would make a logical place for redevelopment that could fund the repair of the landscape.

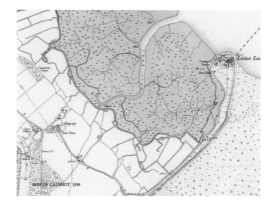

After long consideration, Aldred Drummond has resolved to rebuild the site as a place for marine employment, linked to a new kind of merchant city settlement. The architect Ben Pentreath, the ecologist Jonathan Cox and I are working with a whole design team on a comprehensive scheme that will link the buildings, landscape and natural habitats. The deep dock and basement of the old power station make it possible to bring

boats into the heart of the site and conceal nearly all parking underground. The public spaces and roads on the surface will be for pedestrians and cyclists. Businesses, houses and commercial areas will be concentrated around the dock in the centre of a high-tech new town, but the southern quarter of lower density houses can follow the pattern of New Forest villages established over the last thousand years or more. Pigs, ponies and cattle will roam the streets and open spaces, grazing on the native grasses, acorns and beech mast. It is an ancient way of combining settlement with animals, now more reminiscent of Transylvania than southern England, but one that makes the New Forest one of the most popular places to live in the whole country.

The power station was built on the flat land beside the sea, much of it reclaimed from the intertidal zone. The earlier coastline can be picked out in the wooded ridge to the west, though quarrying for sand and gravel has scarred this landscape too. The project makes it possible to repair the wider landscape as part of the open space for the settlement. The quarry will be restored with a long, raised, chalk serpentine walk that shelters a series of traditional dew ponds on acid grassland, grazed by cows. The wooded scarp will be replanted and contain wild play areas. The old Ower farm will be revived as a dairy and farm shop, providing fresh local food for the new settlement and linking back into the wider estate. The hillside to the south of the farm will be terraced with allotments for both the new Fawley Waterside settlement and the neighbouring village of Calshot. The farm and allotments will link directly to the heart of the town down a foot and cycle path aligned on a view to the dock and the sea. The large buildings on the edge of the dock will have market gardens on their roofs. Food, health, habitation and employment will all fit together as something very new that also echoes a more integrated way of life from centuries ago.

OPPOSITE The sand and gravel quarry that will be restored as a series of dew ponds with a curving raised walkway.

BELOW Aldred Drummond's vision for the new development at Fawley Waterside with a marine merchant city around a dock created from the power station cellar. The housing will take its character from the surrounding New Forest so that ponies and cattle can graze freely along the roads between the dwellings.

Ben Pentreath's plan for
Fawley Waterside.

Primary
School
2ha

Calshot

The landscape sketches planning the integration of the new town with the wider natural and farmed environments.

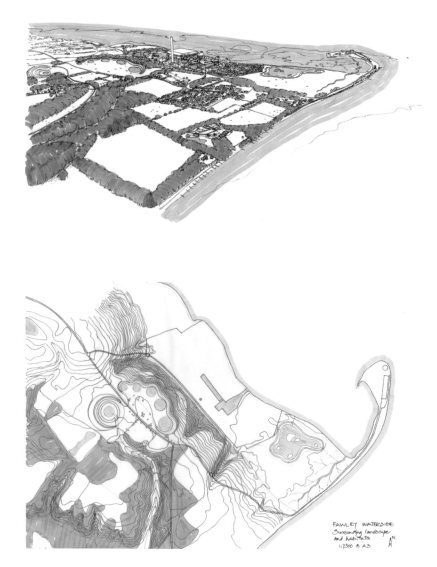

FAWLEY WATERSIDE
Surrounding landscape
and habitats
1:7500 @ A3

The new settlement has the major advantage of connecting directly with thousands of acres of natural and farmed landscape in its hinterland — all under one ownership that takes long-term stewardship seriously. Wrong turns in one century can be reversed in the next. The deep wooded valleys that define the estate and connect the New Forest to the sea will be replanted, grazed and managed as continuous natural wildlife and landscape corridors. The agricultural land will be brought back into traditional mixed rotational farming that revives the soil and tends the livestock. Good food will be grown on the estate and, in combination with the market gardens on the roofs of the boat stack and supermarket, sold directly in the new settlement. The urban and rural communities will be connected and mutually supportive.

OPPOSITE A computer image of the new dock in the centre of the merchant city.

BELOW Buckler's Hard in the New Forest, the inspiration for the grazed glades that will run through the new houses.

MADINAT AL IRFAN

OMAN

On the other side of the world, in Oman, I was asked by the architects Allies and Morrison to work with them on the concept for a completely new city for quarter of a million inhabitants in the desert. They were keen for the plan to be led by the landscape. Water is key to any desert settlement and I was also fortunate to work with Ian Carradice, the water expert at Arup. Topography and hydrology have guided where buildings should go and the local climate and culture have determined the characters of the city spaces that link everything together.

Oman lies on the edge of the tectonic plate where Africa ripped apart from Eurasia 600 million years ago. The geology and botany along this line are extraordinary and the landscape has generated a particular personality

BELOW The dry wadi site for a new city in Oman.

OPPOSITE The diverse Omani native vegetation and natural life that comes with water.

and identity for the country. It is a place where rocks, water and plants have been translated into beautiful agricultural terraces and where farming and date palms are central to the national culture.

The site for Madinat al Irfan captures the resources of this natural landscape. Located between the Hajar Mountains and the Arabian Sea, the city will be founded in open desert with a deep wadi running through its centre. Wadis are dry, rocky valleys formed through millennia of storms into ephemeral stream beds. Moisture is mostly protected below the ground but seasonal downpours bring flushes of vegetation and water to the surface.

The natural landscape has shaped the masterplan for Madinat al Irfan from the very beginning. It was decided to make the most of the topography, keeping the steep slopes open and positioning buildings on the upper, flatter land. The wadi will stay undeveloped as a central open space, with the metropolitan core on the northern ridge and the satellite urban villages on the southern rim. Inhabited bridges, cooled by the valley breeze, will connect the two sides and look out over the wadi landscape.

Water is the source of life in this desert region. The Omani landscape underpins social and legal systems which are fundamentally based on the passage of water through human settlements. The ancient falaj irrigation network of mud-walled channels distributes water by gravity through each farm and town. It is a system that dates back at least five thousand years and communities are organized around very specific access to this supply through

an intricate system of sluices. The falaj are collectively owned and guarded by watchtowers.

The attention to topography in siting the buildings in the masterplan is exemplary, but the treatment of the open spaces that define the character and layout of the city is revolutionary; it revives a tradition that goes back thousands of years to the cities of Mesopotamia and the Hanging Gardens of Babylon. The city will grow its own food using its own water. The steep slopes of the wadi sides will be sculpted into terraces with stone walls to create an urban agriculture that will permeate the whole of Madinat al Irfan. Terraces are a particularly efficient way of growing food. From the Andes to Indo-China, agriculture first evolved by terracing slopes that collect soil, hold water and irrigate through gravity. It has a practical logic that remains sound in twenty-first-century cities.

With a living, working and visiting population of over 250,000 inhabitants, Madinat al Irfan will generate substantial greywater. The costs of recycling greywater come from pumping long distances and removing nitrates and phosphates. The beauty of allowing gravity to carry the water down through agricultural terraces, with crops that need nitrates and phosphates, is that nothing goes to waste and the costs turn into benefits. By the time the plants have extracted the nutrients and the water has percolated through the limestone to the wadi floor, it is stripped clean for the indigenous vegetation that grows in the valley bottom. We are working with the Oman Botanic Garden, a new development by the Diwan of the Royal Court, to source and grow the native plants that will flourish in the wadi base and create a central park that has walks and shelters through a natural wild valley. It will be a place that is fundamentally part of the Omani landscape, flora and culture.

OPPOSITE The ancient falaj channels distribute water in the most beautiful and efficient way.

BELOW The agricultural terraces at Jebel Akhdar hold soil and water on the steep mountain slopes.

OVERLEAF Madinat al Irfan is designed to use the latest low-carbon technology combined with the deep national traditions of productive terraces and falaj irrigation to create a modern resilient desert city.

Water will snake down the terraced slopes in narrow channels and occasional pools to filter into the rough valley base. Date palms, citrus groves and vegetable plots will give way to wild shrubs and trees in a natural rocky stream bed.

The extent and sinuous form of the wadi will mean that the layers of terraces on its sides will actually add up to a continuous linear length of over 200 kilometres (124 miles). Not only will the terraces echo the beauty of ancient towns like Jebel Akhdar, they will also produce a great deal of food. Oman has a gentle and thoughtful culture where the sophistication of modern prosperity has not divorced people from respect for water and growing food. There is a deep love of date palms and the falaj irrigation system that makes life in the hot, arid climate possible. Creating a city that is based on this respect and these traditions has struck a chord with the people we have met and worked with in Oman. It is a settlement that will intrinsically have emerged from the place, the traditions and the practical realities of keeping a twenty-first-century city resilient, healthy and self-reliant. The changing climate and unpredictability of world economic and political forces put new pressure on cities to be able to fend for themselves in times of uncertainty. For cities larger than Plato's ideal of five thousand inhabitants, total self-sufficiency is probably unrealistic, but taking care of food, water and health makes good sense. The aim is to allow public spaces to work in several dimensions. If parks can help to filter water, clean air and

LEFT The nearby city
of Nizwah shows how
buildings can be protected
by continuous canopies of
date palms.

BELOW Oman is famous
for its geology and there is
great scope to incorporate
stone walls into the design.

grow food, as well as providing spaces for walking and recreation, they give a place a sense of responsibility, pride and identity.

In support of this ethos, the Diwan of the Royal Court has donated twenty thousand date palms to help establish the city. The trees will provide a dominant pattern of productive green shade that connects through the streets, parks and sports areas to the corniche and wadi terraces. Omani cities like Nizwah show how a near-continuous canopy of trees can create the feeling of an oasis within the desert. Minarets, domes and towers emerge from a layer of green. Date palms, combined with falaj water channels and restrained pools and fountains in the urban squares, will create shaded streets and squares where the sound and feel of moisture on the air make the city feel cooler and more welcoming.

The more the inhabitants of a city stroll and linger in the public spaces, the greater the sense of life and well-being. When people can also have contact with the soil and take ownership of growing fruit and vegetables, mental as well as physical health greatly improves. The management of the agricultural terraces will need careful consideration. There is, however, enough space for private allotments, professional farmers, school plots, medicinal gardens and even belvedere cafés and teahouses. Furthermore, during the decades of building the city, it will be possible to give temporary plots to the constction workers, who are often a long way from home with no access to cultivation space.

Madinat al Irfan is an idea for a new kind of city where the plan and architecture have responded intimately and subtly with the underlying topography and landscape. The designs flow from the traditions of the people and the pressures of surviving in a harsh climate through an uncertain century. Our concept for this city is to create a place where it is a pleasure to live and to make a settlement where the inhabitants can take an active part in the spaces that belong to them.

SPIRIT

The spirit of the land carries many names and beliefs. From Mother Earth to ley lines to a biosphere of related habitats, we attribute a connected living wholeness to the planet. Landscape architecture attempts to address this. It reaches beyond the responsibilities and practicalities summed up by Alexander Pope as 'use' to try to grasp the 'genius of the place'. This 'genius' is only partly based in physical characteristics – topography, aspect, climate and vegetation; it also covers the memories and associations that have accumulated in that spot. In other words, it is the personality, identity or spirit of the place.

Franklin Farm, Hampshire.

THIS ACRE OF ENGLISH GROUND WAS GIVEN
TO THE UNITED STATES OF AMERICA BY
THE PEOPLE OF BRITAIN IN MEMORY OF
JOHN F KENNEDY
PRESIDENT OF THE UNITED STATES 1961-63
DIED BY AN ASSASSINS HAND 22 NOVEMBER 1963

JFK MEMORIAL

RUNNYMEDE

The John F. Kennedy Memorial at Runnymede is a great example. It is a charming but unremarkable spot and typical of much of the Thames Valley. A busy road runs through the water meadow down beside the river. The memorial itself is modest: a sequence of fifty meandering, rough-cut steps leading up through woodland to a small glade overlooking the river. On the platform a stone memorial tablet to President Kennedy is inscribed with a quote from his Inaugural Address:

Let every nation know, whether it wishes us well or ill, that we shall pay
any price, bear any burden, meet any hardship, support any friend or
oppose any foe, in order to assure the survival and success of liberty.

Despite the modest normalness of the setting and the simplicity of the stone tablet, this is a place of extraordinary power and beauty. It is charged with deep beliefs of our culture in democracy, equality and freedom under law. The JFK Memorial was inaugurated by Queen Elizabeth and Jacqueline Kennedy in May 1965, just eighteen months after his assassination, and the land that it stands on was given by the British people to the United States of America.

This whole valley has significance. Down below, on an island in the Thames, the Witenagemot (the open-air council of the Anglo-Saxon kings) used to be held; and, on the same island, five hundred years later, Magna Carta was sealed by King John in 1215. The place symbolizes liberty. But there is more going on here than a history lesson. I believe that you could walk those steps without knowing all the stories and still be profoundly moved. The number of feet that have trodden the path and the intensity of the emotions they have felt are somehow tangible. The spirit of a place shrinks time and resonates with everything ever felt there.

To my mind, the JFK Memorial was the finest work designed by Geoffrey Jellicoe, the English landscape architect. His steps follow the slope of the land, avoid tree roots and use 60,000 hand-cut granite setts, laid straight into the soil. The design is such a light touch that you hardly notice that a designer has been involved, and the effect is at once very gentle and subtly strong. It is a comfortable climb that encourages you to concentrate on the trees, the light and the rhythm of walking. You reach the glade unexpectedly and the power of the words is undiluted. The complete simplicity and unpretentiousness of the sequence is in harmony with everything it represents.

INSPIRATION

Inspiration is an interesting process. It can be mapped out as a logical sequence of analysis, consultation and some magic moment of intuition, but I suspect that our minds don't quite work like that. Everything happens all at once; and then the mind chases its tail over and over again. Much of this takes place while you are walking, bathing or staring into space. This is not to say that design and inspiration are somehow mystical and magical; quite the reverse. Our minds work hard on many levels and process information and ideas in a more fluid and coordinated way than a linear diagram can capture.

More interesting still is that, although each project should spring from the personality and priorities of its place, there are some larger identities and themes that touch regions, countries, even cultures. From an early age I have been obsessed with landforms and I seem to have ended up in the right country for the obsession. Sculpting the land is an ancient and very British tradition. The climate, the geology and the topography make soil and grass durable and expressive materials to build in. Since prehistoric forts and chalk carvings, there has been a long story of sculpting the land into sensuous forms, held firm by close-cropped turf. Rain helps to grow abundant grass; sheep and rabbits can keep the surface short and smooth; and the low northern light shows off the subtle shapes.

Early earthworks were carefully placed on ridges or knolls to take advantage of the strategic view and make maximum impact from a distance. Their presence still dominate the landscape millennia later. Even when the earthworks were defensive rather than sacred, such as Maiden Castle, Offa's Dyke or even Palmerston's anti-Napoleon redoubts, they were brilliant land sculptures. Tumuli rising through autumn mist have stirred imaginations from Spenser to Hardy to Ravilious. Viking barrows, sacred circles and earth mazes leave an echoing landscape memory in the national mind.

Ironically, earthforms tend to survive even longer than buildings and are repeatedly reappropriated. Burial mounds, such as the one in Richmond Park, have been reused for hunting high points and communication lookouts. The Richmond Park mound aligns with St Paul's Cathedral and is now named King Henry's Mound. Henry VIII supposedly waited there for the signal from the Tower that Anne Boleyn had been beheaded and he could ride off to marry number three. The Thames landscape was dotted with similar viewing mounds, known as mounts. Francis Bacon built mounts at Twickenham Park in the seventeenth century and during the eighteenth century a whole series of raised earthworks created connecting vistas along the river, notably for Princess Caroline at Richmond Lodge and Alexander Pope at his Thamesside villa.

AVEBURY RING

WILTSHIRE

Avebury Ring is a Neolithic henge monument of three concentric stone circles, constructed around 2600 BCE. Although Stonehenge receives all the Oscars, there is something just as powerful about Avebury Ring, the more so for being quietly unexpected. The village has encroached into the centre of the ring and roads run through the middle. The stones are humbler than Stonehenge, and more quizzical, and sheep munch away over the whole site. Somehow the integration of subsequent life into the rings of stones makes them feel less set apart – more connected to our relationship with the land. Wandering up and down the banks and ditches, without fully understanding the five thousand years of significance, and looking across to the huge Silbury Hill, you feel part of a very long story. There is connection without full comprehension and enormous pleasure in the lumpy geometry of a place that still somehow feels sacred.

RIDGE AND FURROW

LINCOLNSHIRE

There is nothing sacred about ridge and furrow. It is the result of centuries of practical ploughing through the Middle Ages in Britain. From the post-Roman period through to the seventeenth century, regular ploughs turned the soil over to the right and tilled the land clockwise in rectangular strips. Over time, this heaped the soil up into parallel ridges separated by troughs or furrows. Modern mechanical ploughing can till in both directions simultaneously and removes these patterns, but where medieval arable land was turned to pasture, the underlying shapes survive, especially in the English Midlands. The forms are slight, usually no more than 60 centimetres (2 feet) in height between the ridge and the furrow. In most lights the fields look flat, but then suddenly evening shadows or ground frost will pick out a comfortable corduroy stretched over the surface of the land. The beauty of the pattern comes partly from parallel light and shadow over an irregular plane; partly from the surprise of being revealed by a transient moment of weather; and partly from knowing that this subtle form represented centuries of patient tilling of the land that fed generation after generation of settlers. There is a further aspect that especially appeals to me: when I look at land I shrink the scale and imagine running my fingers over the surface, feeling and stroking the shapes. Ridge and furrow feels great to the touch.

LYVEDEN NEW BIELD

NORTHAMPTONSHIRE

There is a strange difference between a ruin and an unfinished building. After a few years they look much the same, but the incomplete building is still full of the optimism of construction, as opposed to the melancholy of destruction in a ruin. Lyveden New Bield is a half-finished stone house that was abandoned in 1605 when Sir Thomas Tresham died and his son became embroiled in the Gunpowder Plot to blow up Parliament. To the side of the house is the garden Sir Thomas was also planning. On an intimate domestic scale, moats, ramparts, mounts and orchards wait, half made, along with the stone building. There is none of the clutter of furnishings, plants or statues – just the purity of grass, stone and water. In the flat Northamptonshire countryside, the empty windows and reflecting canals capture light in the most magical way. It is a place of expectation and imagination, full more of hope than memory.

ROUSHAM

OXFORDSHIRE

I keep returning to three particular gardens from the first half of the eighteenth century: Rousham in Oxfordshire, Claremont in Surrey and Studley Royal in Yorkshire. These places seem to distil landform and water to pure spirit. Rousham manages to be wonderfully domestic. The parkland is grazed by longhorn cattle and chickens scatter in the stableyard as you search for the honesty box to pay to enter the garden of what is still the Cottrell-Dormer family home. I first visited Rousham very early on a perfect summer morning. There was no one else around and I was able to amble along the narrow serpentine paths and discover one hidden surprise after another. The grounds were designed by Charles Bridgeman and then overlaid by William Kent. The strength of Bridgeman's design, suspending the gardens above the River Cherwell, gives a clarity that enabled Kent to create a series of delightful eddies in the flow. Kent was evoking the themes of Augustan poetry and classical Arcadia, but you don't need to know any of this to enjoy his temples, pools and grottos. The best of all is a narrow stone rill that meanders gracefully through woodland before flowing into an octagonal reflecting pool in a glade above the river. The subtlety of the light on the slightly turbulent rill calms into a mirror plane in the reflecting water of the octagon. The rill and pool are set in bare, swept earth under trees.

CLAREMONT

SURREY

Kent also followed Bridgeman at Claremont, though the scale is much grander. When I first saw an illustration of Bridgeman's grass amphitheatre for Claremont, I thought the artist had had problems with the perspective, but it really is like that. Grass terraces fan and curve over 1.2 hectares (3 acres) in the most extraordinarily bold shapes and planes. Bridgeman carved in earth and turf the way that a sculptor chisels wood or stone. To the east of the amphitheatre, Kent made a beautiful serpentine ha-ha but unfortunately he naturalized the octagonal pool that Bridgeman designed at the base of the amphitheatre. The concentric rings of the grass terraces descending to an octagonal reflecting lake must have been very powerful when they were first made.

STUDLEY ROYAL

YORKSHIRE

The moon ponds at Studley Royal are serene distillations of geometry and reflection. The simple shapes are cut cleanly out of turf, deep in the valley of the River Skell, and reflect the trees, temple and sky in fractured patterns. The best way to approach Studley Royal is from the cascade to the south. The perfect proportions of the framing lodges and cascade lead you on to the moon ponds, and it is only having glimpsed the ruined Fountains Abbey to the north that you should progress from the sculptural balance of the eighteenth century to the rugged destruction of the sixteenth. The whole sequence shows the relationship between water, landform and philosophy. Studley Royal was created by John Aislabie after his disgrace in the South Sea Bubble financial scandal. Aislabie's expulsion from Parliament and disqualification from public life released him to create one of the finest gardens in England.

The Temple of Piety, seen across the moon and half-crescent ponds at Studley Royal.

TAKING A WALL FOR A WALK

CUMBRIA

The historic examples of inspiration are mostly to show the depth and variety of the earthwork tradition in the British Isles. But earthworking is still very much alive. Some of the most imaginative new directions have been led by environmental artists such as Andy Goldsworthy and Richard Long. Andy Goldsworthy's *Taking a Wall for a Walk* in the Grizedale Sculpture Park, for example, humorously combines memory of the old field patterns with a sensuous form that weaves between the trees and land. Over centuries, the open Cumbrian hillsides had been painstakingly groomed of stones that were collected into walls to contain sheep. As the fields at Grizedale fell into neglect, the walls began to collapse and larch forests were planted. The forest was then turned into a sculpture park. Andy Goldsworthy wove all three histories together in the most simple and imaginative way.

I first saw Andy Goldworthy's work in the Serpentine Gallery in the 1980s. Although I have spent my life looking at nature, Andy Goldsworthy always makes me see things completely afresh. From understanding the ephemeral delicacy of leaves and twigs to the rough beauty of ice and rock, he has managed to keep the open eyes of childhood that you lose with age. And he carries on exploring and imagining and helping us to see. His representation of the San Andreas Fault at the entrance to the de Young Museum in San Francisco's Golden Gate Park has the same subtle wit and beauty as *Taking a Wall for a Walk*. Goldsworthy absorbs history, use and spirit and retells the story with an almost innocent, humorous insight. This is poetry and landscape and observation at their most direct and unselfconscious.

Drawn Stone, Andy Goldsworthy's portrayal of tectonic fracture.

I have given a very personal reaction to these inspiring places, but Bridgeman's landforms at Claremont, set beside Aislabie's moon ponds at Studley Royal, reveal a tradition that has re-emerged more generally in contemporary landscape design, such as Charles Jencks's and Maggie Keswick's work at Portrack, and is now inspiring mounds and earthworks throughout Europe. In the United States, earthworks have also drawn on a separate tradition of native American design. The materials, scale and light are often different, tending to work with massive rock projects in desert areas. Robert Smithson's spiral jetty and the work of James Turrell continue to inspire. Some earthworks in the United States are also clothed with grass, very much in the English tradition. At his farm in Maine, James Pierce consciously drew on burial mounds, military redoubts and turf mazes to create a series of sculptural earthworks. And Maya Lin's work, from the Vietnam Veterans' Memorial to the Storm King Wavefield, is breathtaking.

PALEY PARK

NEW YORK

In addition to its earthworks, the United States has been a major source of inspiration to me. I was fortunate to study under Michael Laurie at the University of California in Berkeley and the works of Thomas Church and Dan Kiley still excite me. But one particular place stands out above all the rest. When I was eighteen, I visited New York. I had travelled to London on a few occasions, but this was the first time I had really been in a full-on city. By the third day, my head was exploding. A friend took me down East 53rd Street and then suddenly off the street into Paley Park. I felt rescued. That was probably the moment I decided to become a landscape architect – although I had no notion that the profession existed and didn't realize what had happened until nearly five years later. The space is only 390 square metres (4,200 square feet), the footprint of one of the buildings that William Paley replaced with a private park, open to the people. The design is incredibly simple – granite setts on the ground, walls of ivy and falling water, a ceiling of honey locusts, Bertoia wire mesh chairs and a few brightly planted concrete pots – yet the place is tranquil, alive and an amazing refuge in a supercharged city. Designed by Zion & Breen in 1967, this is probably still one of the most innovative urban spaces in the world.

LANDFORM

Sculpting the earth is one of the most dramatic and yet playful ways of designing in the landscape. The subtlety of the form, often hidden in flat light, can become powerful at dawn or dusk or in frost and low mist. Combined with different patterns of grasses, grazing or mowing, the scope for imaginative design will keep me absorbed for the rest of my life.

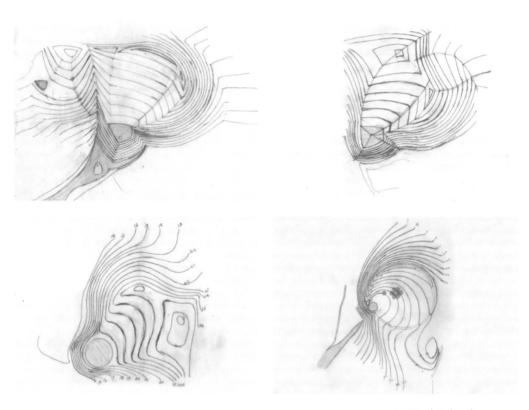

ABOVE Sketches for landforms at Knepp Castle.

HEVENINGHAM HALL

SUFFOLK

BELOW AND OVERLEAF
The fan of grass terraces
behind Heveningham Hall
responds to the flow of the
land, retains the old trees
and gives the house room
to breathe.

One of my first projects, Heveningham Hall, involved massive movements of soil. Behind the house the land rises sharply to the south and the garden front has always posed a problem. Even the brothers La Rochefoucauld, visiting shortly after construction at the end of the eighteenth century, complained that was an unsuccessful space. A typical Victorian parterre had been built on the site in 1877, but the scale and ornamentation jarred beside the 80-metre (260-foot) Georgian façade and retaining walls blocked the views from the main reception rooms. The registered garden beside the Grade I listed house was clumsy for its setting, shaky in its foundations and, to be honest, not very good design. In a ground-breaking decision, English Heritage consented to demolition of the parterre and replacement with a completely new garden of sweeping grass terraces.

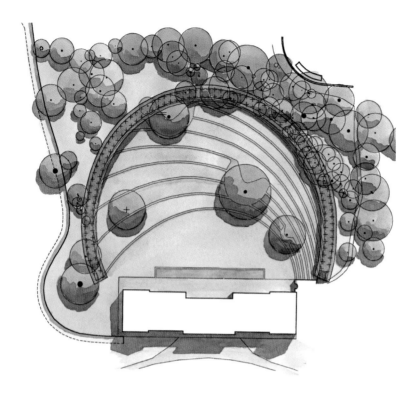

LEFT The design is based on the flow of the golden section spiral, rising 9 metres (30 feet) to the south-west, enclosed by an arc of holm oaks and connected to the house terrace by a 50-metre (165-foot) reflecting pool.

RIGHT Sketch plan for the wider Heveningham estate at Cockfield.

BELOW The swimming pool formed in an old sand pit at the neighbouring hall of Sibton, part of the Heveningham Estate.

Sketching away on the draughting table, I designed a symmetrical pattern of grass steps, responding to the purity of the house. But on returning to the site, it was clear that the underlying slopes were doing something quite different. The ground rises at an angle off to the south-west and cuts back to the service yard beside the house. After a lot of puzzling, I let the land lead the design. The terraces flow with the rising ground, fanning out in a golden section curve. The geometry is broken by grassy domes over the root plates of the veteran trees – oaks and cedars – that predated the parterre. A symmetrical arc of holm oaks shade the walk that contains the terraces and retains a balance with the house, rising gently with the natural slope and descending down steps into the service yard to the west. A 5 x 50 metre (16 x 165 foot) reflecting canal links the house terrace to the lawns and makes a great lap pool. The design was inspired by the landform, the setting of the hall and the scale of the landscape. It has tried to shed the mistakes of the past and yet respond to the needs and memories of the place.

Over the last thirty years, the estate has expanded to include fragmented holdings to the south east, encompassing Sibton Park and Cockfield Park. The creation of lakes in the valley bottoms and terraced landforms on the slopes has continued. At Sibton a sculpted-earth swimming pool has been made in an old sand pit and at Cockfield the chalk quarry will be emptied of rubbish and reprofiled around the limes and sycamores that have established on its banks.

COCKFIELD HALL
Landscape masterplan
1:3000 @ A3

GREAT FOSTERS

SURREY

At Great Fosters the problems were different. Great Fosters has had many lives: from a moated seventeenth-century Windsor Great Park hunting lodge; to one of the houses that belonged to the family who adopted Jane Austen's brother; to an aristocratic lunatic asylum; to the first country house hotel on the Ascot and debutante circuit, celebrated by Noël Coward in *Relative Values*. The elaborate Arts and Crafts gardens have been lovingly restored by the owners, but in 1972 the M25 amputated the last third of the axial avenue and exposed the Grade I building to the noise and fumes of the congested motorway. The whole garden focuses to this vista and the place felt ripped apart.

After years of discussions with the Highways Agency and acquisition of the neighbouring fields, we were able to find the funds to build 800 metres (half a mile) of protective earth bunds and a grass amphitheatre 6 metres (20 feet) high as the new terminus to the avenue. The sculptural landform reduces the noise and hides the motorway at the same time as giving a focal end to the axial vista. To celebrate the opening we held a concert with a string quartet, just 25 metres (82 feet) from the busiest section of motorway in the country. The acoustic was perfect.

The restored Arts and Crafts garden at
Great Fosters where the axial vista had been
amputated by the M25 motorway in 1972.

LEFT AND BELOW LEFT
The vista seen from
both directions. At the
truncated end rises a grass
amphitheatre, flanked by
an 800-metre (half-a-mile)
long bund to conceal the
motorway and protect the
garden from the traffic.
The acoustic is so good
that string quartets can
play only 25 metres (82
feet) away from the traffic.

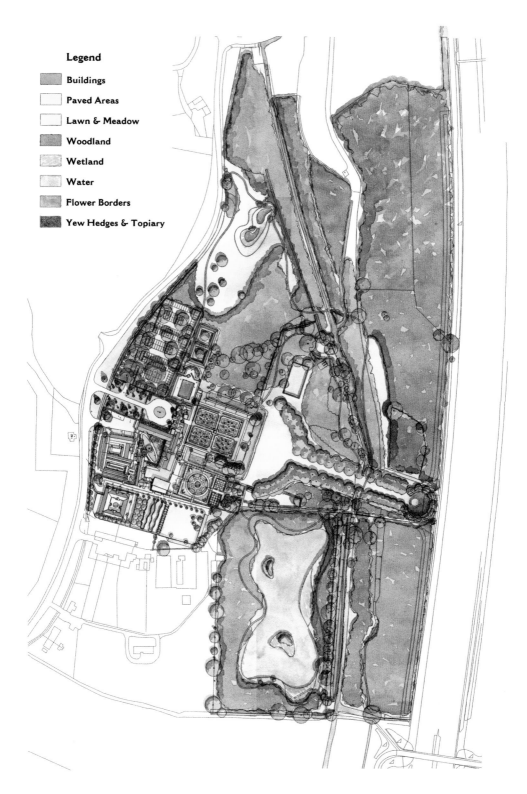

Legend

- Buildings
- Paved Areas
- Lawn & Meadow
- Woodland
- Wetland
- Water
- Flower Borders
- Yew Hedges & Topiary

BELOW The Holker Hall car park has been folded into the land to hide the cars from the wider landscape.

HOLKER HALL

CUMBRIA

Holker Hall is spectacularly sited in the southern Lake District on the edge of Morecambe Bay. The house has been in the family since 1756 and is still lived in by the Cavendishes, descendants of the 1st Earl of Burlington. The estate has survived as a lively modern enterprise, open to the public and working energetically with its woodland, venison, salt marsh lamb and slate quarries.

The parkland stretching down towards the bay is particularly fine and Lord and Lady Cavendish have created a famous garden around the house with rare collections of trees and shrubs. The visitor car park and shop, however, sat rather awkwardly on the slope above the house in a broad expanse of asphalt that reached almost to the front door.

In 2000 I was asked to help produce a long-term masterplan for the grounds around the hall. The first and most urgent step was to tackle the unfortunate car park. Working with the characteristic topography of the parkland, we created a woodland bowl for the cars, scooping up a huge fold of land to separate the parking from the house. The drive was realigned to approach the hall more gracefully

and the visitor entrance diverted to flow in a series of gently rising loops through the trees. We were able to take advantage of the Burlington slate from the estate and create sinuous parking areas of green slate mulch with riven slate details along the road edge.

The car park now feels as though it sits more peacefully on the ground and the sculptural curves create glades of oak trees that have become popular for picnics. Even the most utilitarian of spaces can be attractive if it flows sympathetically with the land beneath, rather than dominating the setting.

The family house has evolved through fashions, fires and family taste and its garden has changed in step. The family continues to alter and refine the garden layout. The latest project was to remove an unfortunate nineteenth-century roadway that sliced through the middle of the garden. The road was perplexingly incongruous. It started and finished in nothing and cut across the flow of the rest of the garden. In its place we have returned the land to its underlying slopes and moulded the space into a cupped grass glade, with a glimpse out towards Morecambe Bay. The glade is surrounded by limes, eucryphias and bulbs, and forms a kind of pagan grove on the meandering circuit around the garden.

BELOW The new pagan grove at Holker Hall creates the imprint of an egg in the grass and is surrounded by a special collection of limes, eucryphias and bulbs.

RIGHT The new car park is the first stage in a major masterplan to rejuvenate the redundant estate buildings as part of an enterprise to support the hall through its own produce of organic venison, salt marsh lamb, timber and slate.

Key:

Existing building

Proposed new build

Existing tree

Proposed tree

Proposed contours

THE HOLT

HAMPSHIRE

Many houses built in the seventeenth century were careful to position themselves in the lee of the south-westerly prevailing wind, tucked under north-east-facing slopes to protect them from the weather. As the houses became grander, heating easier and glass more affordable, the fashion for views and southern light changed priorities. The houses that had been sited for sound environmental reasons found their gardens did not work for the new relationship with the outdoors. A number of places, such as Claremont, took the radical decision to demolish the old house and rebuild on the high sunlit ridge. For others, including Heveningham, the houses were altered and walled gardens were constructed off to the side, but the main south-facing gardens remained compromised and overshadowed by steep slopes.

The Holt is a lovely seventeenth-century, six-bay house overlooking parkland, with its garden tucked into a steep slope at the back. Over the years attempts had been made to carve out tennis courts and random level areas in the looming ground to the south and east, but this had emphasized rather than eased the awkwardness of the setting. Extensions to the house had exacerbated the problem with ground levels over half a metre (20 inches) above the internal floors. Three hundred years after the house was built, the current generation decided to try to sort the problem properly.

In order to give the house space to breathe and make room for generous stone terraces, we had to move huge amounts of chalk. The design creates two descending wings of fanned grass terraces, intersecting in a zigzag that leads up to an old wrought iron gate through perimeter yews. The wings mimic a bird in turning flight, with the zigzag as a spine. The curving terraces make a form of amphitheatre where plays are now performed each year for charity.

RIGHT The new grass terraces carved out of the land behind the seventeenth-century house.

OVERLEAF The south-eastern slope was drawn back to allow light and space to the garden front of the house.

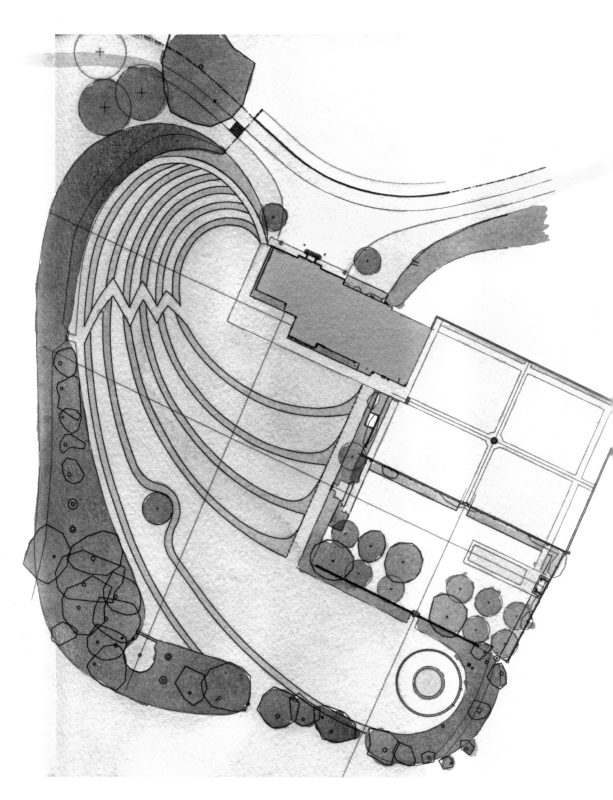

The pattern rotates around the house. The grass terraces descend into a zigzag path that links the library door with the gate to the viewing mound. The design is based on the wings of a bird wheeling in flight.

LEFT The mound with the radial avenues.

BELOW LEFT The terraces in winter frost.

BELOW The terraces in summer with the chalk wild flowers allowed to grow long on the banks.

OVERLEAF A midsummer performance for children: *The Emperor's New Clothes* – in the rain.

Just beyond the grass terraces, the owner's grandmother, who had ambitious plans to expand the formal gardens, had laid out the initial stages with a series of avenues radiating from a circular space. Harnessing this framework, we used the chalk spoil to make a 5-metre (16-foot) high spiral grass mound at the centre of the avenue glade. As you walk up the mound, you look along each avenue in turn and then survey the whole scene from the top, emerging into the setting sun. The most recent project has been to plant a further avenue radiating off the mound terminating with a circular dew pond in a clearing deeper into the woods.

I have managed to stay in touch with all of my earthform projects over the years. The places and the owners have become good friends and it is a joy to watch them evolving together. At The Holt, Ted and Katherine Wake took the decision to let the banks grow long during the summer, just mowing the flat levels of the terraces. On the thin chalk, sprinkled with local wildflower seed, the result has been beautiful. Harebells, quaking grass and mignonette wave gently in the wind and give the formal terraces a softness that hums with crickets and grasshoppers. The winter frost and low autumn light create very different patterns from the same sculptural form.

ROTHERFIELD PARK

HAMPSHIRE

Rotherfield is one of the most perfect English parklands. The great stone house looks east over rolling chalk downland, accentuated by clumps of trees and an arched stone bridge that connects two grassy knolls and makes the entrance to the house. Across the valley, the church is subtly raised on a mound so that the tower rises above the surrounding trees and village. The house itself is the closest thing to a Gothick Scottish castle in southern England and has been used as the location for a number of films.

Although the site is much older, the Grade I house was extensively remodelled in the nineteenth century. Elaborate walled gardens to the north-west are immaculately maintained and the house and parkland have been carefully looked after for generations. Nevertheless, immediately to the south of the house, a rough area of grass sloping up to a southern ridge looked as though the builders had moved out in the 1870s and left the grass to grow over their heaps of rubble. Indeed, this is more or less what had happened. Ambitious schemes for an Edwardian terrace and then a dainty flower garden by Russell Page had never quite caught the imagination or the budgets of the family.

The problem remained that the best garden aspect of the house had never been resolved. The house entrance and approach are on the north front; service yards span the north-west; a dramatic ha-ha revealing views drops away to the east; and yet the main lawn to south remained lumpy and unconvincing.

The solution was to create a generous flat lawn that gives the stables and tower a level bank and base, allowing the architecture on the northern and western sides of the space to be properly grounded and relate formally to the garden. On the southern ridge things could be freer. In carving back the land to create the flat lawn, the slope became steeper and more dramatic. The idea was to curve the grass slope in an arc and to create a rising pleat or grass terrace, a little like a gusset in a Renaissance sleeve. The transition between

The recontoured lawn to the south of Rotherfield Park.
The view opens eastwards to the parkland and church.

the end of the space and the view was more difficult. It needed a form that was strong enough to balance the towers of the castellated house and the stables as well as linking to the bold downland beyond. In the local tradition of earth fortifications and tumuli, we made a great hemispherical mound that acts as a fulcrum between the ridge and the carved slope. The views from the top are spectacular and the turf architecture is bold enough to balance the stone and brick edifices on the other two sides of the enclosed lawn. My only regret is that I didn't carry the rising pleat right up around the mound, like peeling a narrow slice out of an apple. Suggesting that, after the project had been completed and the grass finally bedded down, was not tactful.

LEFT The house and stable block now relate more comfortably to each other.

BELOW A single grass terrace rises to a hemispherical mound in the local tradition of earth fortifications and tumuli.

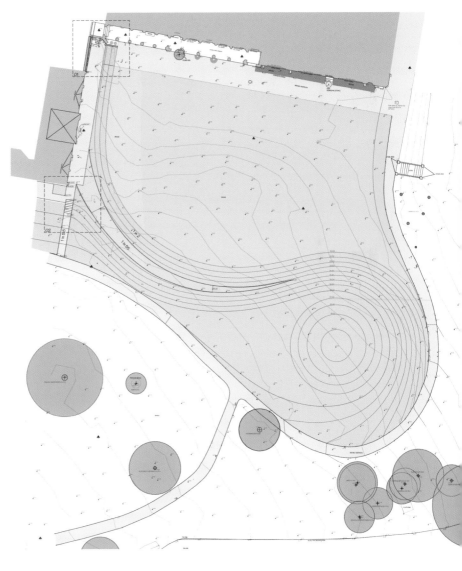

BOUGHTON HOUSE

NORTHAMPTONSHIRE

I was first asked to Boughton on a morning in late spring 2004. Lord Dalkeith showed me the extent of the restoration work that he and his father were undertaking on the avenues and canals in the historic landscape and then led me up to the top of a small hill covered in sycamores and Lawson cypress. From the edge of the hill you could just see down to the crumbling banks of the River Ise and an uneven stretch of land beyond, leading up to a holly hedge and the family swimming pool 800 metres (half a mile) away. 'So what would you do with this?' he asked me.

The overgrown hill we were standing on was originally a perfect truncated grass pyramid, thought to have been designed by Bridgeman in 1724 for the 2nd Duke of Montagu. It looked out over the long view, referred to on old plans as *'the hurried over'* – a sequence of land that had never been fully resolved or designed, leading up to a medieval stew pond and bowling green. It was a thrilling thought: the possibility of working with one of the greatest formal landscapes in England and designing something that was both inspired by the place and its precisely calculated pattern, yet excited the next generation.

Boughton is a sculptural landscape of avenues, canals and grass terraces created by the first two Dukes of Montagu between 1685 and 1725. The first quarter of the eighteenth century in England was one of the most stimulating stages in the history of landscape design. During the transition between the intricate formality of French baroque and the broad panoramas of English parkland, there were some bold experiments with sculptural and geometric landforms.

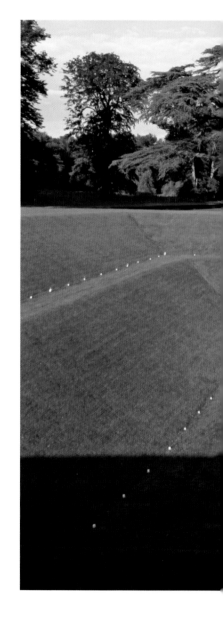

RIGHT AND OVERLEAF The new landform at Boughton, responding to the 1724 pyramidal mound and the precise geometry of the early eighteenth century. The idea was to juxtapose an Orphean Hades with the Olympian Mount, designing the intervening ground plane to symbolize civilized life on Earth with the patterns of the classical golden section.

These were quickly smoothed away by the Arcadian English Landscape Movement and not many survive. Bridgeman was the leading designer of those two remarkable decades and Boughton is one of the few of these transition landscapes to escape intact from subsequent design fashion. While the family concentrated on their great Scottish estates, they left the place to fall asleep. It was not until nearly three hundred years later that the Dukes of Buccleuch began to reawaken and restore the landscape. It is a garden of land and water, avenues and vistas, rhythm and reflection.

Although many of the landscapes we most enjoy are the results of eccentric and inspired individual patronage, few opportunities now arise to work with a really imaginative patron on this scale in a landscape of this importance. Institutions and committees are generally too cumbersome and diluted to commission really innovative work. The simple question on the hill was an intense moment and I am not sure what answer was expected, but it came to me in a flash. Rather than make a rival mount or competing structure, I replied: 'Why not go down rather than up?' I suggested inverting the pyramid across the river and digging a mirroring hole that descended the mount's 7 metres (23 feet) below the ground. Amazingly, we went on from there.

Two immediate challenges became apparent: hydrology and archaeology. Digging a 50 x 50 metre (165 x 165 foot) hole down 7 metres (23 feet) beside a flowing river has some inherent problems. The house and garden are also listed at Grade I, so every millimetre of the project had to be checked for archaeological remains. We were fortunate in an exceptional team: Brian Dix on the archaeology, Miles Waterscapes on the very precise construction and Mott

BELOW The precise mathematical layout of Boughton in the 1720s, possibly by Charles Bridgeman. The mound and axial 'hurried over' run up through the centre of the drawing.

BELOW RIGHT The acoustic 7 metres (23 feet) below ground is perfect for music and has become a place of art and performance within the elegant landscape of the grounds.

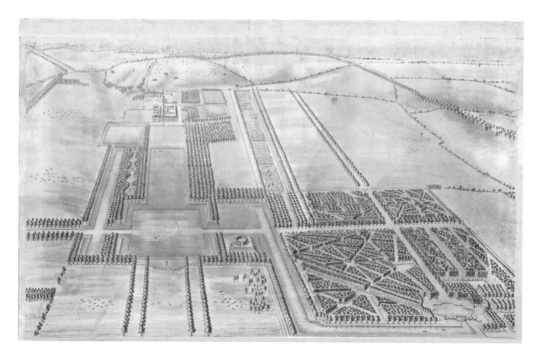

Macdonald on the engineering – all coordinated by the remarkable landscape manager at Boughton, Lance Goffort-Hall. After some initial nail chewing, the archaeological concerns calmed down. It turned out that the area had indeed been '*hurried over*' and the remnants of a minor earlier parterre had been lost in dredging activity during the previous century. The engineering issues too were resolved by a seam of finest blue clay beneath the surface, which meant that the landform could be constructed as a kind of reverse reservoir to keep the pressure of the groundwater from bursting through. English Heritage and the local authority were exacting but very helpful, and the whole thing was built within a year of starting and opened in a classic English downpour.

The seventeenth/eighteenth-century layout of the Boughton landscape is based on the most precise mathematics. Studying the axial rhythm of squares within the wider geometry of the landscape, some interesting patterns and relationships emerged. The mount and empty rectangle of land across the river form perfect golden rectangles: the classic proportions observed by Vitruvius, Hadrian, da Vinci and Corbusier in creating harmony between man and geometry. Bridgeman was a keen observer of these rules and his designs for Kensington Palace Gardens, as well as Boughton, are revealing when Vitruvian Man is superimposed on the plans.

The harmonic proportions are based on the perfect relationship between a square and a rectangle. Whenever a square is inserted into the golden rectangle, a rectangle of exactly the same proportions remains. The rectangle/square relationship can subdivide infinitely, creating a beautiful spiral as each of the squares' corners are connected. The golden section spiral is similar to

Charles Bridgeman was an expert in the use of the
proportions of the golden section. It is interesting
to superimpose Vitruvian Man on his design for
Kensington Palace Gardens (BELOW LEFT) and
indeed on the combination of the mount and
Orpheus (BELOW RIGHT AND BOTTOM).

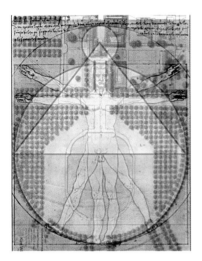

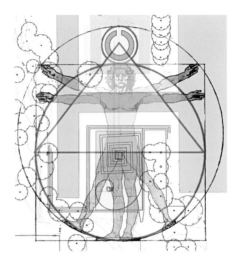

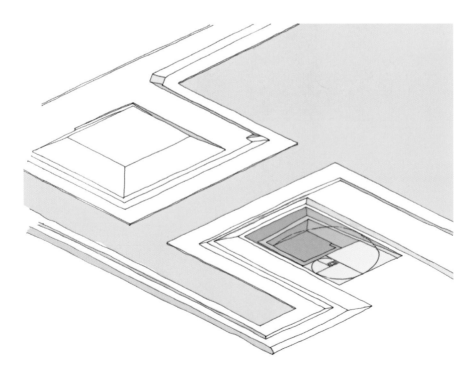

the Fibonacci series spiral, but the pattern is more precise as it is based in geometric form rather than numerical sequence. The geometry discovered in the existing garden has been a guiding principle for the inverted pyramid. The rhythm of squares is followed and linked by a spiral rill of water, which then translates into a gentle grass path that descends to a square reflecting pool at the base of the inverted pyramid. Spring water, from the source at the lily pond 800 metres (half a mile) away, bubbles up in the centre of the spiral and then flows down into the lower pool before returning to the river. As a final exploration of the perfect geometries, a polished 4-metre (13-foot) steel cube pops up into three dimensions on axis with the medieval pond. Its burnished surface glows with the setting sun.

The new design continues the materials of Boughton: grass, stone, oak and water. The grass slopes of the inverted pyramid match the mount in angle and character and the grass ramp that spirals down to the lower pool is graded to 1 in 40. The reflecting pool is contained by the same oak as the canals to give a clean turf edge to the water. The golden section paths, rill and upper pool are cut by the local estate stonemasons to mark the pattern within the turf. The land between the inverted pyramid and the lily pond is being managed for the fritillaries and wild flowers that thrive there. The longer grass is mown into four squares of 60 metres (200 feet) that follow the centre line of the lily pond and create a subtle continuity of axial formality to connect the sequence of square spaces, from the upper

BELOW At the very beginning of the golden section spiral, spring water bubbles up and flows out along the rill and across a reflecting square of water towards Orpheus. Above the square of water a polished steel cube is positioned for art installations. It has nozzles for dry ice mist or can be covered by material for light shows.

lawn down to the mount. Specialized remote-controlled banks mowers enable the team of gardeners at Boughton to keep the entire grass and water landscape in crisp simplicity.

Walking around the landscape, the new design is deliberately invisible, but drawing near to the mount, you catch sight of the grass path that spirals down and through the pool of still water deep underground. The water reflects the sky, a little like an inverted James Turrell occulus, to create an Orphean Hades to complement the Olympian Mount. The earthwork came to be named after Orpheus to capture its descending form and as a place for music and contemplation. When Orpheus' wife, Eurydice, was killed by the bite of a serpent, he went down to the Underworld to bring her back. His songs were so beautiful that Hades finally agreed to allow Eurydice to return to the world of the living – until Orpheus doubted and looked back to check that she was really there.

Beneath all the mathematics and engineering, there is a special feeling at Boughton. The clarity and simplicity of the shapes work with shadows and reflections to make a huge landscape of planes of light that show the sky

BELOW Although the Orpheus landform offers its own contemporary drama, it has been deliberately set low to respect the earlier landscape and blend into the greater pattern.

BELOW RIGHT The Olympian mount and Orpheus are placed opposite one another across the canalized Styx-like River Ise.

and space in a fresh way. Orpheus is a surprise. As you come to the lip of the landform, it opens as a vertiginous hole. The sides appear much steeper and the bottom much deeper than they really are. The grass path, however, is on a very gentle incline as it unwinds along the sides of the pyramid. It is 250 metres (820 feet) long and takes some time to descend. As you go down, the air gets stiller and the surface sounds disappear. It becomes quiet and contemplative. Then just as you are nearing the bottom, the square of water brings the sky into clear focus. The path continues to spiral down beneath the water, but there is a moment where you pause on the edge of the water, deep underground, but surrounded by light.

For me that boundary between sky and earth or land and water is a magical pivot of existence. It takes you to a kind of Orphean dilemma, or perhaps to a place of connection with those you have lost who are still really a part of you, and to that perplexing duality of being that can only be grasped through the senses and not fully understood by the mind. Orpheus is now a place for music, for art installations and for parties, but when you are alone there, it is a place to lose yourself in thought.

HURSTBOURNE PARK

HAMPSHIRE

Landforms can be minimal as well as monumental. The house at Hurstbourne Park is the third on the site since the eighteenth century. It sits at the crest of a dramatic chalk valley that descends southwards through wooded parkland. The idea was to connect the house as directly as possible to the views to north and south, keeping more intimate and flower gardens off to the west.

An old ha-ha provided the perfect transition to the southern parkland but there was a desire for some relief between the house terrace and the ha-ha. It was important not to interrupt the view and so I proposed a subtle knot garden of turf cut down into the grass. It is only really in morning and evening light that the shapes of the garden emerge as a modern sculpture, but it is a good place for children to roll and play, and blends easily with the scale of the valley beyond.

A gentle turf knot garden
(BELOW, with its model,
OPPOSITE) makes the
transition between the house
and its parkland.

COUNTY HALL

LONDON

On an even smaller scale, the courtyard of the old County Hall has been similarly transformed. The old concrete roof grate in the centre of the court was turned into a turf sculpture. Weight restrictions led to some unorthodox use of polystyrene as subsoil and growth mats for vertical grass faces, but the final result was a kind of ziggurat of turf in a hard and austere urban space.

I reinstated the old 1930s system of suspending a central light off wires from the building and the turf sculpture glows green through the archway from Westminster Bridge. Sadly, now artificial turf has been substituted for grass, but the effect from a distance is still good.

The turf sculpture at the entrance to the former County Hall in London.

LEFT The model of the landform between the factory and the road.

BELOW LEFT The first concept sketch of the scheme.

BELOW RIGHT The mounds being formed as the factory was still under construction.

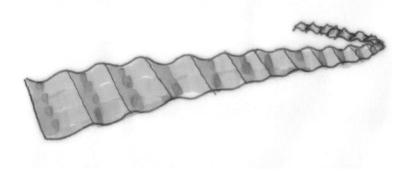

VITSŒ FURNITURE FACTORY

LEAMINGTON SPA

Mark Adams, the managing director of Vitsœ, and his artist wife, Jennie Moncur, are visionary perfectionists. Every tiny detail of their new factory at Leamington Spa has been beautifully considered – right out to the landscape.

The site at the entrance to the town was challenging. Sandwiched between arterial roads, roundabouts and the railway, it is set on steep slopes above the traffic. Taking the cue from the local agricultural landscape, the slopes have been corrugated into a grass landform that fans from steep perpendicular ridges and furrows at the north-western corner of the site, to gentler oblique furrows as it wraps around to enclose parking along the southern boundary.

The earthform has been seeded with a local wildflower and grass mix, which is allowed to grow long on the ridges and is mown lower in the furrows to emphasize the shape. The aim is to graze the slopes with sheep after the hay has been cut in late summer. It was a pleasure to develop the idea of a free-flowing landform alongside Mark and Jennie's precision. Peter Wilder patiently took the concept into working drawings.

In the first year, the landform was covered in poppies.
Perennial wild flowers have now taken over and the aim is to
graze sheep on the slopes after taking a crop of hay each year.

FRIARS STILE ROAD

RICHMOND

My old studio in London had a small walled garden with a roof terrace overlooking Richmond Park. I grew vegetables and herbs in copper planters around a big glass block table that doubled as a roof light for my desk underneath. I also had fun with the walled garden below. The lawn was sculpted into shallow wave forms, with foaming Yorkshire fog grass on their crests. The idea was that – with a bit of stretched imagination – the view from the terrace looked out over breaking waves, pulsing in from the dark-blue recycled-glass parking area.

The roof terrace (FAR LEFT) above the studio in Richmond. The glass table doubled as a roof light for my desk.

On the ground floor the studio linked to a jetty walkway that caught the lunchtime sun. I worked with the sculptor Ben Barrell to design a big blue bench that five of us could sit on in the sunshine. It followed Ben's wonderful hydro-dynamic lines and fortuitously mimicked the shape of the sycamore helicopters that fell from the tree above.

OPPOSITE, LEFT AND RIGHT
Shallow waves of snowdrops
advance on the studio from a
car park of recycled blue glass.

BELOW The bench by Ben
Barrell was designed for us all
to sit in the lunchtime sun.

FRANKLIN
FARM '90

HOME GROUND

Growing longer in the tooth encourages you to take stock. What has made a difference and what has been achieved? Landscape has such a mind and dynamic of its own that I suspect wondering about achievement is just not relevant. You cannot control land like a building; and a good part of the pleasure is seeing the wayward growth and changes that are made by the people and wildlife that inhabit each project. On wider environmental issues the forces of politics, climate and financial fictions leave the best of intentions stranded in rock pools. You can only hope that accumulated homeopathic drops of good sense might help to infuse the system.

The privilege, therefore, of being able to manage your home ground during a lifetime is very special. To grow up with trees that you have planted; to wait for the swallows to come back each spring and the barn owls to fledge each summer; to raise a herd of cattle from a single cow; to grow your food and fuel; to experiment and change your mind; to share and argue about it all with an equally stubborn partner – these things make life worth living. Montaigne had it down when he wrote, '*I want death to find me planting my cabbages, but careless of death, and still more of my unfinished garden.*'

Franklin Farm, Hampshire.

FRANKLIN FARM

HAMPSHIRE

My grandfather first heard about Franklin Farm when it was about to be bulldozed to the ground; my parents were able to buy the ruined farm buildings and slowly rescue them from collapse. For nearly a thousand years there had been a consistent pattern of settlement on this land, owned and tenanted by Titchfield Abbey and then, after the dissolution of the monasteries, by the Earl of Southampton. Agricultural fortunes rose and fell up to the First World War, when the loss of life left a number of the farms unmanned. Many holdings were then amalgamated and the farmhouses divided up to form labourers' cottages. After the Second World War, a number of these houses were completely abandoned. Franklin Farm was one.

The farm sits on gentle downland that has a long history. There is a Bronze Age barrow, the remains of an ancient British village and a group of Iron Age tumuli. Although the farm had originally been made of assarts cut from ancient woodland, by the time we found it, all the trees had been felled and the abandoned house and barns squatted rather forlornly on the edge of a huge and apparently flat arable field. The spot nevertheless still had a real atmosphere of peace and for us as children it was heaven. In Middle English a 'franklin' was a free man rather than a serf and the farm was specially noted for being tenanted by a free man (the rent in the Middle Ages was a pound of cumin at Michaelmas). Some of that sense of calm independence seems to be an intrinsic part of the place.

Franklin Farm is an old settlement on the Hampshire downs not far from the coast.

LEFT The ponds freshly
dug on the edge of the
pasture stay full from
rain and dew and are
now bubbling with toads
and insects that bring in
the swallows.

BELOW LEFT The cows
habitually gather at the
ha-ha for a scratch at
cocktail time.

BELOW The sunken spiral
with a sculpture by Simon
Thomas curls out into the
field and up towards
the mound.

OVERLEAF The sunken
spiral curves out through
the field to a small mound.
From the top of the mound
you can see Tennyson
Down on the Isle of Wight.

Gradually the house was made habitable and a long series of experiments with the land began. Twenty-eight years ago we managed to buy back some of the farmland and I planted over four thousand trees to restore the enclosure and protection from the Channel winds. My partner, Pip, and I now live here and are breeding a herd of longhorn cattle. We have unpicked the 1960s rescue work and rebuilt the panels within the old oak frame, cutting and weaving our own hazel for wattle and digging up our chalk for daub. We started our herd of English longhorns with Faith, Hope and Charity. Faith turned out to be bad-tempered and Charity had narrow hips, but Hope has gone on to be the matriarch of the entire herd. Rotating grazing with haymaking and combining cowpats and chickens have transformed the soil and its insect life.

Restoring chalk meadows and planting woods is a slow but wonderful process. A bald arable field sprouts a bristle of tree tubes and then nothing seems to happen for a while, except the voles and mice move into the tubes and the area becomes patrolled by barn owls. Then one spring, green shoots appear out of the tubes and, before you know it, real trees start to break the horizon. I planted 4 hectares (10 acres) of wood to follow the gentle contours of the land and curve around curious dimples in the surface. As the trees have grown up, the shadows pick out the form of the valley and the dimples have been turned into dew ponds. Woodland flora has seeded itself under the closing canopy, starting with vetches and crosswort and progressing to primroses, helleborines and orchids.

The insects, birds and mammals have multiplied and the field of grim oilseed rape has reverted to a complex community of buzzing, singing and burrowing. The wood is now twenty-seven years old and we have already started thinning and coppicing, not only for the hazel wattle but also to stoke the woodchip boiler that fuels all the buildings on the farm.

The farm walls and buildings have created a series of protected yards following two alignments. The fourteenth-century house and cow byre are aligned north–south looking down the valley towards the sea, whereas the nineteenth-century barns splay a little on the east–west axis. Immediately beside the house is the old circular dew pond. Collection of rain and dew in dry chalk valleys was always important. The circle of the pond and the gentle curving forms of the valley have led to a serpentine ha-ha and fence line. East of the house we cut an Archimedes spiral down into the chalk, curling in towards a sculpture by Simon Thomas. The spiral then rises up and unfolds out into the field to reverse direction and climb a small spiral mound (I experimented on all these forms at home myself before risking them on clients). From the top of the mound you can just see to Tennyson Down on the Isle of Wight. My dog is buried in the mound and I will join him there one day.

A vegetable garden and orchard are wrapped around the kitchen. The farmyard, chickens, turkeys and ducks are off to the north-east in a second courtyard. Flint is everywhere. Each bed has to be sieved and the fields have

BELOW The original dew pond right beside the farmhouse was essential for watering stock on the dry chalk. It is now patrolled by a family of moorhens who manage five hatchings a year.

BELOW RIGHT The vegetable garden and orchard between the kitchen and the farmyard.

OVERLEAF Flint and chalk are everywhere, in the walls, in the paving and in every precious kilo of topsoil that you have to sieve and feed to grow anything.

to be picked of monster flint stones. So the walls, the paving and the ha-has are made from the ubiquitous rock. Flint is still something of a geological mystery but the current theory is that it is a sedimentary cryptocrystalline formation created by water flowing through chalk. When the flint is knapped, or broken in two, the halves open to a black glassy centre surrounded by a white rim. Bound together in walls with lime mortar or in paving with crushed chalk, the flint produces a very tough black and white surface that reflects a silver light and glistens in rain or dew. Construction in flint is particular to the geology of parts of southern England and it is a joy to rediscover old techniques and invent new uses for this site-specific rock.

There is a sense of being a continuing part of three thousand years of settlement here. The Bronze Age barrow slumbers to the east. The Saxon hearth became a chimney in 1620 and we continue to gather around the same fire in the evening, tend the woods, graze the downs and harvest water and vegetables in a way that this thin chalk soil can support. For all our technological advances, there are some fundamental relationships with the soil that persist. The tumuli have inspired new earthforms; the flint has shaped new paving and walling patterns; and the field and woodland boundaries have evolved with farming methods and view lines. But, deep down, we are still a sequence of settlers cooperating with the land, cohabiting with wildlife and drawing inspiration from the spirit of the place.

INDEX

NOTE: page numbers in **bold** refer to captions to the illustrations.

ACKNOWLEDGEMENTS

The full title of this book should probably be Led by the Land and the People in It. There have been many good friends who have directly and indirectly helped me to write this book. My mother, my sister and Ilse Treurnicht gave me the courage to make the first leap and become a landscape architect. Since then Pip Morrison has kept me grinning and grounded with sceptical support and Welsh enthusiasm.

My professor at Berkeley, Michael Laurie, and my fellow classmates, especially Louise Mozingo, Valerie Remitz, Anna Kondolf and Mark Adams, helped to turn excited curiosity into determination. I am grateful to Richard Flenley, who gave me my first job as a landscape architect, and to the excellent people who have passed through my practice, starting with the irrepressible Marco Battaggia and continuing through Poppy Evans, Eva Henze, Peter Wilder, John Goldwyn, Max Askew, Tessa Walliman Taylor, John Dawkins, Jeremy Rye, Chris Connor, Simon Rackham, Christina West and Grania Loughnan.

There are some particular people that I would also like to thank. When I first set up on my own, Mavis Batey and Gilly Drummond gave me tremendous support. Along the way I have had some great conversations which helped to plough directions through my lumpy thoughts with Laura Beatty, David Attenborough, John and Ben Gummer, Jane Parker, Janet Richmond, Grania Cavendish, Carla Carlisle, Graham Harvey, Merrick Denton-Thompson, Alan Titchmarsh and Dieter Helm. I am particularly grateful to Dieter for writing the foreword. I have also been fortunate to work with some brilliant architects who have become good friends: Níall McLaughlin, Graham Morrison, Alex Lifschutz, Terry Pawson, Ben Pentreath and William Smalley. And lastly the infinitely patient Jackie Hands has made all of my models and Rob Orford has been an invaluable guide through all my earthworks with his genius digger driver, Colin Mortlock.

John Nicoll showed great perseverance in getting me to write the first book and Emma O'Bryen, Becky Clarke, Jo Christian and Penelope Miller at Pimpernel Press have patiently steered me through this second edition.

Special acknowledgements are due on each of the projects:
Solovki: The Prince of Wales Business Leaders Forum, Susan Causey, Elizabeth White, Artyom Parshin and Brian Dix
Transylvania: The Mihai Eminescu Trust, The Prince of Wales's Charitable Foundation, Jessica Douglas Home, William Blacker and Nat Page
Thames Landscape Strategy: Sherban Cantecuzino, David Coleman, Sir David Attenborough, Lord Deben, Jason Debney, Ken MacKenzie, Donna Clack, Jenny Pearce, Mavis Batey, David Lambert, Henrietta Buttery and Mike Dawson
Longwood Gardens: Paul Redman, Sharon Loving, Rodney Eason, Stu Appel, Alex Michaelis, FMG and Kate Donnelly
Villa La Pietra: New York University, Bob Berne, Ellyn Toscano and Nick Dakin-Elliot
Moscow Apothecaries' Garden: Dmitri Schvidkovsky, Sergei and Georgi Gevorkyan, Artyom Parshin and Alexi Retejum
Oxford Botanic Garden: The Friends of Oxford Botanic Garden, Louise Allen and Piers Newth
Winchester water meadows: Jeff Hynam, John Wells, Robin Chute, Peter Wilson, Rue Ekins and Graham Roberts
Shawford Park: Peter and Bettina Mallinson, Peter and Christian Douglas, Peter Glyn Jones and Bruce Guest
Heveningham Hall: Jon and Lois Hunt, Argus Gathorne-Hardy, Graham Broadhurst, Rowena Francombe, Grahame Sutherland, Peter Holborn and Anne Westover
Natural History Museum: Níall McLaughlin, Tilo Guenther and team, Peter Wilder, Expedition, Thomas Matthews, Atelier 10, Justin Morris, Ian Owens and Fiona McWilliams

V&A: John Madejski, Gwyn Miles, Stephen Doherty, Mark Jones, Moira Gemmill and Jane Lawson
Hyde Park Corner: English Heritage, the Royal Parks, Westminster City Council, the Crown Estate, the Grosvenor Estate, the Royal Household, Transport for London, DCMS, CABE, Australian and New Zealand High Commissions, Philip Davies, John Barnes and Drew Bennellick
Hyde Abbey Garden: Friends of Hyde Abbey Garden, Winchester City Council, Hampshire Gardens Trust and especially Barbara Hall, Ken Qualmann, Dick Winney and Tracey Sheppard
Maggie's Swansea: Laura Lee, Marcia Blakenham, Charles Jencks, Diego Teixeira Seisdedos, Terra Firma and Ed Coveney
City of London Cemetery: Corporation of the City of London, Ian Hussein, David Lambert and Margaret Cooke
Chelsea Barracks: Quatari Diar, Jeremy Titchen, Stephen Barter, Sarah Raven, Michael Squire, Jeremy Dixon and Edward Jones
Fawley Waterside: Aldred and Fiona Drummond, Ben Pentreath, Jonathan Cox, John Adams and Nicole Yip
Madinat al Irfan: Graham Morrison, Alfredo Caraballo, Sowmya Parthasarathy, Ian Carradice, Phil Denton and Ed Gant
Great Fosters: The Sutcliffe family, Richard Young and Russell Dixon
Holker Hall: Hugh, Grania and Lucy Cavendish, Duncan Peake, Yvonne Cannon and Mark Carroll
The Holt: Ted and Katherine Wake
Rotherfield Park: James, Judy, Arthur and Emily Scott
Boughton House: The Duke and Duchess of Buccleuch, Lance Goffort Hall and Chris Sparrow
Hurstbourne Park: Nick and Tal Fane
County Hall: Stuart Guest
Vitsœ Furniture Factory: Mark Adams and Jennie Moncur

All the photographs are by Kim Wilkie and the drawings are copyright © Kim Wilkie with the exception of the following:
Allies and Morrison p134; Artyom Parshin p16,19; Barbara Hall p104; Bruce Guest pp67,68; Ben Pentreath pp123,125,126,128,129 Cameron Maynard p157 bottom; Duke of Buccleuch p184; English Heritage p72 top; Geoff May p171 top; Hampshire Wildlife Trust p58; Higher Perspective pp168,171 bottom,177,182,189,205; Michael Squire and Partners p117; Mark Adams pp195,197; National Trust ©NTPL/Andrew Butler p148; Níall McLaughlin pp41,42,43; Peter Douglas p64; Private Collection p147; Robert Orford p72 bottom
Tate Britain ©Tate, London 2011 p30 top; V&A Museum p93; Winchester College pp60,61

Pimpernel Press Limited
www.pimpernelpress.com

Led by the Land
First published in 2012 by Frances Lincoln Limited
This revised edition published in 2019 by Pimpernel Press Limited

Copyright © Pimpernel Press Limited 2019
Text © Kim Wilkie 2012, 2019
Photographs © see above

All rights reserved. No part of this publication may be reproduced, stored in a retrieval system or transmitted, in any form, or by any means, electronic, mechanical, photocopying, recording or otherwise, without prior permission in writing from the publisher or a licence permitting restricted copying. In the United Kingdom such licences are issued by the Copyright Licensing Agency, Barnard's Inn, 86 Fetter Lane, London EC4A 1EN.

A catalogue record for this book is available from the British Library.

Typeset in Bliss
ISBN 978-1-910258-52-1

Printed and bound in China
9 8 7 6 5 4 3 2 1